North Africa AD 533–36

COMBAT

Byzantine Cavalryman
VERSUS
Vandal Warrior

Murray Dahm

Illustrated by Giuseppe Rava

OSPREY PUBLISHING
Bloomsbury Publishing Plc
Kemp House, Chawley Park, Cumnor Hill, Oxford OX2 9PH, UK
29 Earlsfort Terrace, Dublin 2, Ireland
1385 Broadway, 5th Floor, New York, NY 10018, USA
E-mail: info@ospreypublishing.com
www.ospreypublishing.com

OSPREY is a trademark of Osprey Publishing Ltd

First published in Great Britain in 2023

© Osprey Publishing Ltd, 2023

A catalogue record for this book is available from the British Library.

ISBN: PB 9781472853707; eBook 9781472853691;
ePDF 9781472853714; XML 9781472853684

23 24 25 26 27   10 9 8 7 6 5 4 3 2 1

Maps by www.bounford.com
Index by Rob Munro
Typeset by PDQ Digital Media Solutions, Bungay, UK
Printed and bound in India by Replika Press Private Ltd.

Osprey Publishing supports the Woodland Trust, the UK's leading
woodland conservation charity.

To find out more about our authors and books visit
www.ospreypublishing.com. Here you will find extracts, author
interviews, details of forthcoming events and the option to sign up for
our newsletter.

Artist's note

Readers may care to note that the original paintings from which the
colour plates in this book were prepared are available for private sale.
All reproduction copyright whatsoever is retained by the publishers. All
enquiries should be addressed to:

info@g-rava.it

The publishers regret that they can enter into no correspondence upon
this matter.

Author's note

The Byzantines considered themselves Roman. Consequently, in the
sources we find Procopius writing about the Roman forces and I have
occasionally followed him in this. I have also followed Procopius'
spellings of Vandal names as well as the names of several Roman
commanders of *foederati*. In several cases there are many, similar,
alternatives for names and I have given an indication of what those
are at the first occurrence of a name. Some of the place names used by
Procopius remain unidentified, but where these are known for sure (or
where there are theories as to their locations) I have given the modern-
day equivalents. Procopius uses both 'Massagetae' and 'Huns' as terms for
the Huns (I have stayed with Huns throughout) and he also uses 'Moor'
for the Berber peoples of North Africa – I have adopted the latter for all
references to Moors in the sources although I have used 'Libyan' to refer
to the local population when Procopius does so.

Procopius begins his accounts of several battles with (sometimes
lengthy) speeches. Unlike many ancient historians who include speeches
in their accounts which they cannot possibly have heard, Procopius was
at least present (certainly for the speeches given by Belisarius and perhaps
some others) and so renders a more believable account. His relationship
to Belisarius was such that he could also have had access to any notes
that existed. This marks him out to be (perhaps) believed even more than
other eyewitnesses to history who did not have such access but may have
heard real speeches and who then wrote them down at length – claiming
they are verbatim or convey a sense of what was said. Even so, we must
still be cautious as speeches before battles were a long-established literary
trope, giving historians the opportunity to break up their narrative, offer
alternative theories on a subject or simply show off their rhetorical skill
and training; or add drama to what might otherwise be straightforward
narrative. We should keep this in mind for all of Procopius' speeches,
even though some of the material included might be entirely genuine and
may reflect words actually spoken by Belisarius and other commanders.

CONTENTS

INTRODUCTION   **4**

THE OPPOSING SIDES   **10**
Army composition and recruitment • Organization and command
Tactics and equipment

AD DECIMUM   **29**
15 September AD 533

TRICAMARUM   **41**
15 December AD 533

THE BAGRADAS RIVER AND SCALAE VETERES   **57**
AD 536

ANALYSIS   **70**
Byzantine effectiveness • Vandal effectiveness

AFTERMATH   **74**

BIBLIOGRAPHY   **77**
Sources • Ancient works • Modern works

INDEX   **80**

Introduction

In June 533, the Byzantine Emperor Justinian I (r. 527–65) launched the first of his campaigns to reconquer the Western Roman Empire. This was not to be a campaign in Italy but in North Africa – modern-day Tunisia, Algeria, Libya and Morocco – conquering the Vandal kingdom that had been in place there since the early 5th century. This war pitted one of the greatest Byzantine generals, Belisarius, against the Vandal king, Gelimer (or Geilamir, r. 530–33). Our best source for the war is the *History of the Wars* by Procopius of Caesarea, a participant and eyewitness. He begins his *Vandalic War* (books 3 and 4 of the eight-book *History of the Wars*) with a long account of the rise of the Vandals (3.1.1–9.26).

The Vandals had established themselves in North Africa in the early 5th century AD and their empire included not only North Africa, but Sardinia, Corsica and the Balearic Islands. The empire was founded by Gizeric (or Gaiseric, or Genseric, r. 428–77) who was ruler of both the Vandals and the Alans. Under his rule, the Vandals had invaded North Africa from Spain in 429, taking Carthage in 439 and establishing a powerful empire. They sacked Rome in 455, plundering it for 14 days (hence the modern-day use of the word 'vandal'), and had repulsed a previous Roman invasion in 468. A treaty of perpetual peace was agreed with the Romans in 476. Gizeric's son, Honoric (or Huneric, r. 477–84), used the title 'King of the Vandals and Alans' for the first time and, as a sign of his people's growing power and influence, he married Eudoxia, the daughter of the Western Roman Emperor Valentinian III (r. 425–55).

Honoric was an unpopular king and was succeeded by his eldest male heir and nephew, Gunthamundus (r. 484–96). The succession of the eldest male relative was the rule put in place by Gizeric. Gunthamundus was succeeded by his brother, Tarasmundus (or Tharasmund, r. 496–523), who married the daughter of the Ostrogothic king, Theoderic the Great (r. 475–526), who ceded Lilybaeum (modern-day Marsala, Sicily) as a dowry. As a result

The Barberini ivory (now in the Louvre, Paris, Inv. OA 9063) shows a triumphant Byzantine emperor as a cavalryman. It could represent Justinian I (r. 527–65), or his predecessors Zeno I (r. 474–91) or Anastasius I (r. 491–518); candidates range from Constantine I (r. 306–37) to Heraclius (r. 610–41). He wears a muscled cuirass, *pteruges*, cross-laced *cothurni* boots and a cloak, and wields a spear. The more elaborate medallion decorations to his horse's trapping match those of the ivory plaque on page 14. Immediately behind the emperor's horse and in the bottom panel are represented bearded western barbarians (wearing trousers, boots and leading a lion); these may represent Vandals, Ostrogoths or perhaps Franks (the back of the ivory is inscribed with a list of Frankish kings). The caps of these figures (which look similar to Phrygian caps) may argue against this, however, suggesting Scythians. The barbarians on the right of the bottom panel represent men from the East (with elephant and tiger). The panel on the left contains a bearded senior officer, possibly a general or consul (and conceivably Belisarius), likewise wearing a muscled cuirass with *pteruges* and a cloak; his long *spatha* scabbard is also visible and his hairstyle suggests he is of barbarian stock. This figure carries a statuette of victory; above the emperor the angel crowns him with the palm of victory (this has broken off). In the top panel, Christ looks down flanked by angels. Produced in Constantinople (modern-day Istanbul, Turkey), the iconography well suits the victories over the Vandals and the 'Endless Peace' with Persia. (Azoor Photo/Alamy Stock Photo)

of this, the Vandal Empire reached its greatest and most powerful extent under Tarasmundus. He maintained good relations with the Eastern Roman Emperor Anastasius I Dicorus (r. 491–518).

By the beginning of the 6th century, the Vandal navy was a piratical threat throughout the Mediterranean. Moreover, the Vandal population, adherents of the Arian faith since the 4th century, also actively persecuted Nicene Christians, the faith of the local inhabitants of North Africa. Persecutions occurred principally under Honoric (after a period of toleration) and his successors Gunthamundus and Tarasmundus, although persecution was ended by the latter.

On Tarasmundus' death in 523, the kingship passed to Hilderic (or Ilderic, or Childeric, r. 523–30), son of Honoric and Eudoxia. As a result of his lineage, Hilderic maintained good relations with the Eastern Roman Empire. Procopius calls him 'a very particular friend and guest-friend of Justinian' (3.9.5), even before the latter acceded to the throne in 527. Unlike the majority of Vandals and their rulers, however, Hilderic followed the Nicene, orthodox faith of his mother. This led to the conversion of many Vandals, which caused consternation among the Arian Vandal nobility and Arian priests. Hilderic was not interested in military matters and left these to his nephew, Hoamer, whom Procopius calls 'Achilles of the Vandals' (3.9.2).

In 530 the pro-Roman Hilderic was deposed in a rebellion led by his cousin, Gelimer. One reason for this rebellion may have been a massive defeat suffered by the Vandals at the hands of the local Berbers, a setback referred to only in passing by Procopius (3.9.3); victory was an important factor in Vandal leadership. Gelimer replaced Hilderic, re-established the priority of the Arian faith and had Hilderic and Hoamer – and Hoamer's brother Euagees (or Hoageis) – imprisoned in Carthage. Gelimer then resisted Justinian I's requests to have his prisoners sent to Constantinople (modern-day Istanbul, Turkey). Hoamer was later blinded (3.9.14). Gelimer was the eldest male heir after Hilderic and so was set to inherit the kingship; Hilderic was also probably aged over 60 when he acceded to the throne, and childless.

Gelimer's seizing the throne led to several rebellions against Vandal rule. In Sardinia the Gothic governor Godas revolted, and the city of Tripolis (modern-day Tripoli, Libya) broke away; Lilybaeum too had been retaken by the Visigoths after the Vandal mistreatment of Tarasmundus' widow Amalafrida. The usurpation of Justinian I's friend Hilderic's throne also led to an ultimatum from Constantinople, demanding Hilderic's release and threatening that if this did not happen, the treaty which had existed between the Romans and the Vandals since 476 would be null and void. Gelimer responded by stating that the matter was none of the emperor's business. Incensed, Justinian I planned an ambitious invasion to be launched from Constantinople.

What we now know as the Byzantine Empire still saw itself as the Roman Empire in the 6th century, the inheritors of the empire that had been split into two parts, Eastern and Western, during the late 3rd and 4th centuries. With the fall of the Western Roman Empire to the Ostrogothic kingdoms in 476, the inhabitants of the Eastern Roman Empire simply continued to refer to themselves as Romans.

Coming to the throne in 527, Justinian I faced many wars during his long reign, and the Vandalic War is now seen as the start of his ambitious *renovato imperii*, the attempted re-conquest of the former Western Roman Empire to restore the Roman Empire to its former territorial limits. Justinian I's Germanic general, Flavius Belisarius, would be integral to those ambitions. Procopius makes it clear (3.10.2) that the invasion of North Africa was Justinian I's idea and one that was met with opposition from his advisers. Procopius tells us that

> every one of the generals, supposing that he himself would command the army, was in terror and dread at the greatness of the danger, if it should be necessary for him, if he were preserved from the perils of the sea, to encamp in the enemy's land, and, using his ships as a base, to engage in a struggle against a kingdom both large and formidable. (Procopius, *History of the Wars* 3.10.4)

One of those who opposed the idea of the expedition seems to have been John the Cappadocian, who stated (3.10.14) that the journey to Africa

would take 140 days and claimed that it would take a whole year for news of the campaign to reach Constantinople. Persuaded by the dream of a bishop, however, Justinian I put his plan in place and appointed Belisarius to command. As soon as the Persian War was concluded with the signing of the 'Endless Peace' in September 532, Justinian I must have begun planning for the new campaign. Belisarius' force, only 10,000 infantry and 5,000 cavalry drawn mostly from the allied states, the *foederati*, set off in June 533.

On 22 June 533, Belisarius set sail from Constantinople in a fleet of 500 ships, heading for Heraclea (near modern-day Eriklice Köyü, Turkey), spending five days there, then Abydos (near modern-day Çanakkale, Turkey). Four days were spent there due to a lack of wind. From there the fleet headed to Sigeum (modern-day Kumkale, Turkey), then Malea (either the modern-day town of Akhlia or Cape Agrilia, both on the island of Lesbos, Greece), then Taenarum (modern-day Cape Matapan, Greece) and Methone (modern-day Methoni, Greece), where Belisarius was met by reinforcements who had marched there by prearrangement with Constantinople. From Methone Belisarius sailed to Zacynthus (modern-day Zacynthos, or Zante, on the island of Zakynthos, Greece) before crossing to Sicily. This took 16 days due to light winds. He probably made landfall on the east coast, although it is not recorded where, and the fleet proceeded to Caucana (modern-day Porto Lombardo or Kaukana, Sicily) before crossing to the islands of Gaulus (modern-day Gozo) and Melita (modern-day Malta) and moving on to North Africa with a strong wind.

Belisarius landed in North Africa in September and made camp one day's march from Syllectus (modern-day Salakta, Tunisia; Procopius 3.16.9) at a place Procopius calls 'Shoal's Head' (3.14.17). The most likely place for this landing was at Cape Vada (modern-day Ras Kaboudia, Tunisia) and the (modern-day) town of Chebba. From Syllectus, Belisarius marched to Leptis (or Leptis Parva, modern-day Monastir, Tunisia), then Hadrumentum (now a suburb of the city of Sousse, Tunisia) and reached a place called Grasse, 350 *stadia* (64.8km using 185m per *stade*; 73,8km using Procopius' 211m per *stade*) from Carthage. This was perhaps around Pupput (modern-day Hammamet, Tunisia, 81km from Carthage); Sidi Khelifa, Tunisia, 35km south of Hammamet, is an alternative site. The next day's march took them across the base of the modern-day Cape Bon because the land troops worried that the fleet was out of sight on their right (Procopius 3.17.15). There, Belisarius camped 7km from Ad Decimum near Carthage, so the march that day was less than half the average distance Procopius gives us.

Meanwhile, Gelimer was at Hermione, a location which defies identification, but which should be located inland and south of Carthage, probably at Capsa (modern-day Gafsa, Tunisia). Other candidates include Sufetula (modern-day Sbeitla, Tunisia) and Theveste (modern-day Tébessa, Algeria). From there, Gelimer sent a letter to his brother Ammatas in Carthage and set off in pursuit of Belisarius. The next day's march took Belisarius' men to within 10 Roman miles (14.8km) of Carthage, to the site of the battle of Ad Decimum. Gelimer shadowed Belisarius' march, starting at Hermione, catching up with the invading army at Ad Decimum.

After victory at Ad Decimum, Belisarius took Carthage and Gelimer retreated to the Plain of Boulla (probably around the area of Bulla Regia, near modern-day Jendouba, Tunisia). From there the Vandal king summoned his brother Tzazon (or Tzazo, or Zano), who had been sent to reconquer Sardinia. He had

achieved this in record time, but his letter telling his brother of his victories arrived in a Carthage now controlled by Belisarius. When Tzazon learned of Gelimer's defeat, he hastened to North Africa with his entire force, landing on the border between Numidia and Mauretania and then marching to Gelimer at the Plain of Boulla. The newly reinforced Vandal army marched on Carthage in December before withdrawing, pursued by Belisarius.

The armies met at Tricamarum, some 30km from Carthage, around modern-day Oued Ellil, Sanhaja or Borj Chekir, all places on the outskirts of modern-day Tunis and on the Bagradas River. Defeated again, the Vandals retreated to Hippo Regius (modern-day Annaba, Algeria) and Gelimer took refuge on Mount Pappas (probably Mount Edough, near Annaba). The Berber city of Medeos, located near where Gelimer took refuge, remains unidentified.

Belisarius, now in control of all of Vandal North Africa, then sent expeditions to Sardinia, Corsica, Caesarea (modern-day Cherchell, Algeria), the Strait of Gibraltar and the fort of Septem (or Septem Fratrem near Abyla, the modern-day autonomous Spanish city of Ceuta, North Africa). Further Byzantine forces were sent to the islands of Ebusa (Ibiza), Majorica (Mallorca) and Minorica (Menorca). The city of Tripolis (modern-day Tripoli, Libya), which had rebelled from Vandal rule, was reinforced.

Soon after Belisarius' departure for Constantinople in 534, the troops left behind in North Africa mutinied due to lack of pay and poor treatment under Belisarius' replacement, Solomon. He had been one of Belisarius' commanders, sent back to Constantinople in mid- to late September 533 with news of Belisarius' victories. The mutineers chose a former bodyguard, Stotzas (or Stutza), as their leader. The Vandals who joined Stotzas' mutiny in 536 had taken refuge on Mount Aurasium (the Aures Mountains in Algeria and Tunisia), perhaps around one of the peaks in Belezma National Park, Algeria. Belisarius returned to find that Stotzas and his mutineers had marched on Carthage from the Plain of Boulla. The Vandals withdrew and Belisarius pursued them to the site of the unwalled city of Membresa (modern-day Medjez el Bab, Tunisia), near to which the the Vandals encamped on high ground. The best candidate for the high ground is El Aroussia, Tunisia, 10km closer to Carthage.

Defeated, Stotzas retreated to Gazophyla (Gadiaufala, modern-day Ksar-Sbahi, Algeria) where the mutiny continued. The final defeat of the mutineers at the hands of forces led by Germanus, Justinian I's nephew, took place at Scalae Veteres, probably a site in Numidia to which the mutineers had withdrawn. The best candidate is Cellas Vatari (modern-day Faïd es Siouda, Algeria), located south-east of Theveste (modern-day Tébessa, Algeria), a hill some 325km from Carthage, although there are other candidates such as between Madauros (modern-day M'Daourouch, Algeria) and Vasampus (modern-day Morsot, Algeria), which was on the route Stotzas had followed to Carthage from Gazophyla and situated closer to Carthage (some 280km rather than 325km).

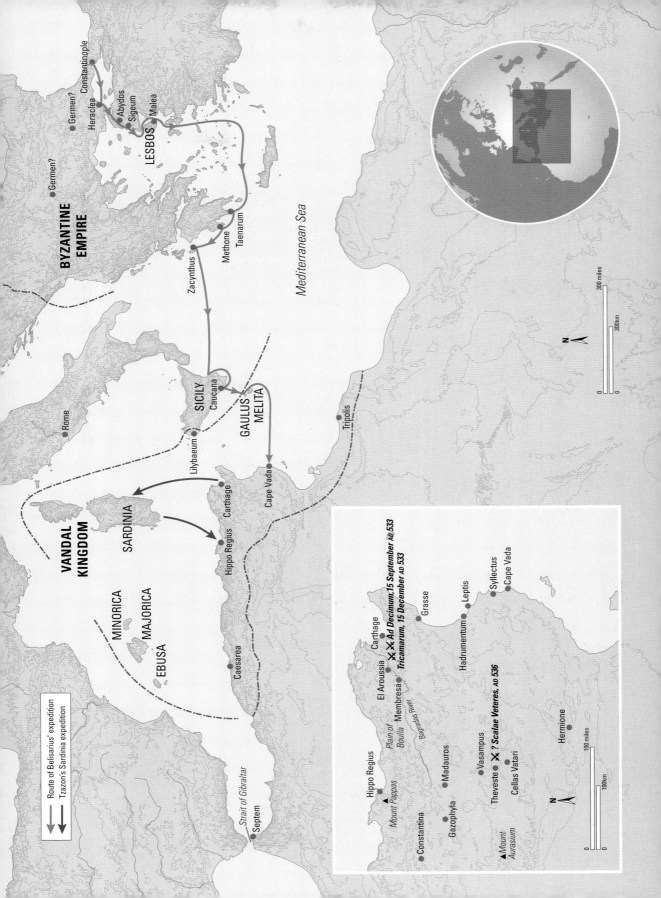

Germen?

Constantinople

Heraclea
Abydos
Sigeum
Malea

**BYZANTINE
EMPIRE**

Germen?

LESBOS

Methone
Taenarum

Zacynthus

Mediterranean Sea

Rome

SICILY
Caucana

Lilybaeum

GAULUS
MELITA

Tripolis

Cape Vada

Carthage

Hippo Regius

**VANDAL
KINGDOM**

SARDINIA

MINORICA

MAJORICA

EBUSA

Caesarea

Strait of Gibraltar

Septem

300 miles

300km

N

Route of Belisarius' expedition

Tzazon's Sardinia expedition

Hippo Regius

Carthage

El Aroussia
Membresa

✗ ✗ *Ad Decimum, 15 September* AD *533*
Tricamarum, 15 December AD *533*

Grasse

Leptis
Hadrumentum
Syllectus
Cape Vada

*Plain of
Boulla*

Bagradas River

Madauros

Vasampus
✗ *? Scalae Veteres,* AD *536*
Theveste
Cellas Vatari

Hermione

▲ *Mount Pappas*

Constantina

Gazophyla

▲ *Mount
Aurasium*

100 miles

100km

N

The Opposing Sides

ARMY COMPOSITION AND RECRUITMENT

Byzantine

Procopius' account (3.11.1–21) of the troops and command structure for Belisarius' expedition is remarkably full of detail, telling us that 10,000 infantry and 5,000 cavalry were prepared at Constantinople, gathered from both the regular troops and the *foederati*, a term Procopius glosses as from the term for treaties, *foedera* (3.11.3-4). These men were provided by allies of the Romans, often on the periphery or outside the empire, bound by a treaty (a *foedus*) and these communities agreed to provide a number of troops for a certain length of service. This kind of agreement had been in place in Roman armies for centuries providing troops called *auxilia* (auxiliaries) but, in the 4th century, *foederati* became the designation of troops formerly known as *auxilia*, especially because the term '*auxilia*' became a designation of regular troops.

Procopius does not, however, seem to use the official designations of units and when he does, these are often incorrect, at least as far as our understanding of how the Late Roman Army was organized goes. The Byzantine army of the 6th century had been inherited from the Late Roman system and therefore consisted of armies of *limitanei* (frontier troops) on the borders (located in a network of fortresses) and *comitatenses* (mobile field armies) that accompanied generals on campaign. In Justinian I's reign there were five armies of *comitatenses*, each commanded by a *magister militum* ('master of soldiers'). Two of the *comitatenses* armies were *praesentalis*, meaning 'in the presence' of the emperor, both located close to Constantinople. Agathias tells us (*Histories* 5.13) that each of Justinian I's armies was 15,000 men strong. A typical Byzantine field army numbered between 15,000 and 25,000 men so Belisarius' command was typical, albeit at the lower end of that spectrum.

Cavalry units typically made up one-third of armies of *comitatenses*, the remaining two-thirds being composed of infantry; Belisarius' force, numbering 10,000 infantry and 5,000 cavalry, offers a perfect example. The *clibanarii* and *cataphractarii* (the heaviest types of cavalry) made up 15 per cent of each army, although we do not know whether Belisarius had this proportion of troops in Africa against the Vandals. The remainder of the cavalry were equipped with bows and thrusting spears. All Byzantine cavalrymen were armed with *spathae* (long swords). Although these men carried bows and could operate as mounted archers, they were not designated as such – that was a role left to units of *foederati* such as those provided by the Huns. Roman cavalry were usually what we might term 'medium cavalry' and capable of charging with their spears or lances.

We do not possess specific details of the units for the army lists that Belisarius brought to North Africa despite knowing a great deal about the contingents of *foederati* involved. Older designations such as *legio* (legion), *cohors* (troop), *vexillatio*

This detail of the San Vitale Mosaic in Ravenna, Italy, shows the bodyguards of Emperor Justinian I. These are either the *excubitores*, *protectores domestici* or the *bucellarii*. Procopius does use the term *excubitores*, although seemingly in the wrong context; otherwise he uses *doryphoroi* (bodyguards) very often to refer to Belisarius' *bucellarii*. We can see the design of the shields clearly (with the Chi Rho design, a monogram of the Greek capital letters ' Χ ' (Chi) and ' Ρ ' (Rho). A second, different design can be glimpsed, perhaps suggesting a second unit. They all carry lances, wear torques and have long hair, the last two features suggesting that they are of Germanic origin, and all wear highly decorated tunics. As this is a 'domestic' scene of such troops, it is difficult to tell whether such men operated as *cataphractarii* or *clibanarii* in combat – the emphasis on their spears may, however, suggest they were *cataphractarii* or *clibanarii*. A single unit of *bucellarii* is listed in the *Notitia Dignitatum*: the *Bucellarii iuniores* – although the exact title is not entirely clear and some manuscripts list them as *Comites catafractarii Bucellarii iuniores*, which may be related to their status as *cataphractarii*. These were a vexillation from the *comitatenses* under the *magister militum per Orientem*; the term *iuniores* implies that there had been a unit of *seniores* at some point. This unit was not, however, a privately raised and paid for unit as they would become, but listed as a regular unit in the *comitatus*. (DEA/A. DAGLI ORTI/Getty Images)

(detachment) and *ala* (wing) were supplanted by *numerus* in Latin or its Greek equivalents, *arithmos* or *tagma*: these simply meant 'unit' or 'number'. Infantry units were nominally 1,000 men strong and cavalry units 500 men strong. These designations applied to regular army troops. Many more forces were supplied by *foederati* – often considered superior fighters (Haldon 2008: 27) – and the prominence afforded them in Belisarius' battle formations perhaps reflects that status.

More prominent still in Belisarius' battles, however, were the *bucellarii* (guard units) that each commander was allowed to recruit. Their name was derived from their ration of biscuit-like bread, *bucellatum* (Nicholson 2018: 270), probably similar to hard-tack. Procopius probably means *bucellarii* when he uses the term 'guards' or 'bodyguards'; he frequently uses the term *doryphoroi,* (sing. *doryphoros*, meaning 'spear-bearer' or 'bodyguard'). The term had become regularly used during the reign of Honorius (r. 393–423) (Olympiodorus F74). The *bucellarii* were equipped and paid for by the commander and Belisarius had more than 1,000 of them in North Africa (Haldon 2008: 27); there seem to have been 1,100 at the battle of Ad Decimum.

A member of Belisarius' advance guard, this man charges forward against the Vandals commanded by Ammatas, Gelimer's brother, coming from Carthage. He landed at Cape Vada only a few days earlier and has proceeded systematically towards Carthage, the Vandal capital. Privately hired, paid and equipped as *cataphractarii*, the *bucellarii* operate as the bodyguard of Belisarius; the general deploys his 1,000-plus *bucellarii* in the most dangerous and important roles. The 300 *bucellarii* charge Ammatas' numerically superior force, trusting that they will win the day or fight long enough for Belisarius, some 4km away with the rest of the army, to ride up.

Weapons, dress and equipment

His primary armament is a thrusting spear (**1**). He is also equipped with a *spatha* (**2**), worn on his left hip, and a composite bow (**3**) and quiver (**4**), as evidence suggests that all Byzantine cavalry were equipped as archers.

He wears a long, decorated tunic (**5**) typical of the age, legwear (**6**) based on that shown in the *Notitia Dignitatum* and boots (**7**). He also wears a cloak (**8**) and an iron-gilt Berkasovo-type cavalry helmet (**9**). He is heavily armoured, wearing a coat of scale armour (*squamata*)

(**10**). In addition to his armour, he carries a shield with an identifying blazon (**11**). It is striking how outnumbered Belisarius' forces often were and yet how easily they bested the vaunted cavalry of the Vandals; this may again argue in favour of the Byzantine cavalry being heavily armoured in comparison to their Vandal foes.

His horse has been provided from the emperor's private stocks from Thrace and wears typical horse fittings (**12**), including a four-horned saddle.

This 6th-century Byzantine ivory plaque shows infantry and cavalry (a horse-archer) led by a dignitary, perhaps the emperor himself. The armour and equipment give us an idea of the similarities in equipment for infantry and cavalry – both troop types wear scale armour with *pteruges* and similar helmets. The horse-archer's helmet does show a crest that is lacking on the infantry's headgear and he seems to wear no cloak (although cavalry of the time did have them). He also shows no evidence of a shield, although cavalry of the time were equipped with shields, spears and bows. The details of horse trappings and furniture are also informative. In several of the battles explored in this book, the infantry played only a minor role – they were either intended as an immovable bloc (usually in the centre) while the cavalry delivered a decisive charge or, in the battles fought by Belisarius, they often did not become involved at all: they did not reach the battlefield at Ad Decimum; and the battle of Tricamarum seems to have been all but decided by the cavalry before the infantry were engaged. The Byzantine infantry were present at the battle of the Bagradas River, although that battle too was decided by cavalry action. At the battle of Scalae Veteres, the infantry were in the centre but the battle was decided, once again, by cavalry action. In many ways, however, decisive cavalry actions against an all-cavalry enemy in the form of the Vandals should not come as a surprise. (Ancient Art and Architecture/ Alamy Stock Photo)

It was the *bucellarii* who delivered the decisive charges in battle, such as by the Byzantine cavalry commander known as John at Ad Decimum (3.18.3–10) and against Tzazon by both John and Belisarius at Tricamarum (4.3.10–13). We do not know how these men were armed or armoured, but it is most likely that they were equipped as *cataphractarii* or perhaps *clibanarii*, heavily armoured and armed with lances and swords, although they may also have had bows. Nonetheless, they were heavy cavalry capable of delivering charges with spears and, if they were armed as *cataphractarii* or *clibanarii*, this would explain their use in such charges and their relatively low casualty rates (only 12 and two at Ad Decimum – and both in encounters where they were heavily outnumbered). A count of 1,000 heavy cavalrymen would indeed make up some of the 15 per cent of forces so armed in armies of the period. Negin and D'Amato (2020: 6–18) argue that Belisarius' *bucellarii* were equipped in this way. The term *cataphractarii* is not necessarily used in our sources either – Ammianus (19.1.2) also uses the term *ferreus equitatus* ('iron cavalry').

Procopius often tells us who the commanders of the *foederati* assigned to Belisarius were although he does not use the equivalent of their rank: *comes* (count). He names Dorotheus and Solomon (3.11.5), the later a eunuch and both a *magister militum* and *praefectus praetorio* (praetorian prefect), although these are terms Procopius does not use. In addition, Procopius names 'Cyprian, Valerian, Martinus, Althias, John, Marcellus' (3.11.6), and the Cyril he mentioned as already sent to Sardinia (3.11.1–2). The commanders of the regular cavalry were Rufinus, Aïgan Barbatus and Pappus (3.22.7). Later, however, Aïgan is called 'Aïgan the Massagete' (3.11.9, 4.10.4). The regular infantry was commanded by Theodorus Cteanus, Terentius, Zaïdus, Marcian and Sarapis (3.11.7), but overall command of the infantry was held by John of Epidamnus (or Dyrrachium; modern-day Durrës, Albania) (3.11.8). The sheer number of commanders named for the expedition is more than we have in other campaigns of the era, but we do not know what units they commanded except when we are told where their troops were from (such as Dorotheus' Armenians). The rest of Belisarius' troops 'were almost all inhabitants of the land of Thrace' (3.11.10); 600 Huns, all mounted bowmen, were led by Sinnion and Balas, while 400 men of the Heruli were led by Pharas (3.11.11). Belisarius was 'followed by many spearmen [*upaspistai*] and many guards [*doryphoroi*] as well, men who were capable warriors and thoroughly experienced in the dangers of fighting' (3.11.19). Procopius here uses the term *upaspistai*, which literally means

'shield-bearers' but is often used to designate spearmen. Procopius, therefore, names five infantry commanders, eight *foederati* commanders and four 'regular cavalry' commanders. If we divide these into units of 1,000 infantry and 500 cavalry we arrive at 5,000 regular infantry, 11 commanders of *foederati* and 2,000 regular cavalry. In addition to Belisarius' 1,000 *bucellarii*, if five of the units of *foederati* were cavalry, with strengths ranging between 400 and 600 men on average, we arrive at Procopius' total of 5,000 cavalry. In addition to the 600 Huns and 400 Herulians, we also find 400 as the number of men commanded by Cyril (3.11.1, 3.24.19). If the remaining six *foederati* were infantry units up to 1,000 men strong (although perhaps weaker), we arrive at Procopius' total of 10,000 infantry.

Other than the Armenians, Huns and Herulians, and men of the 'land of Thrace', neither the nationalities of the *foederati* nor what kinds of troops they were are specified. Bury (1889: 76) considers that the *foederati* were all cavalry although he concedes (127) that some of Belisarius' infantry may have been drawn from them. MacDowall (2016: 121), perhaps following Gibbon (1788: 624) and Bury (1889: 127), adds the 600 Huns and 400 Herulians to Procopius' total rather than have them as part of the count. In which case, Belisarius had 6,000 cavalry. More recently, Merrills and Miles (2014: 232) considered that Belisarius had 18,000 men.

Vandal

We have much less information on the organization of the Vandal forces than we do for the Romans, even if we collate that information from widespread sources. Some clues come from references to the loyalty of men to their commander, such as Tzazon's separate address to the men who had accompanied him to Sardinia before the battle of Tricamarum (Procopius 4.2.24–32). Gelimer's brother Ammatas (or Ammatus) had men in Carthage before the battle of Ad Decimum who may also have been men who owed their loyalty

Two views of a Late Roman iron cavalry helmet. This example (in a private collection in the United States) has hinged cheek pieces; as the cheek pieces cover the ears, this seems to indicate it was a cavalry helm. This is a much plainer example than others that have been discovered and perhaps represents a lower level of investment by the wearer. In more elite units we can expect more decoration like those examples found at Deurne, the Netherlands, and Berkasovo, Serbia. This helmet could still have had a crest attached. In the frontal view, we can see that the two halves of the domed cap are joined to a central ridge by rivets with a brow band offset by horizontal ribs. The nose-guard and ornamental arching brows are riveted to the brow band, and the cheek pieces are flanged toward the neck and hinged to the brow band, each piece perforated below the chin, the neck-guard with an everted hemispherical flange hinged to the back of the brow band. Height 27.5cm, weight 1,426g. (INTERFOTO/Alamy Stock Photo)

Detail of a late-5th- or 6th-century silver plate, found in Isola Rizza, Italy, and now in the Museo di Castelvecchio, Verona (Inv. No. 13871). The armoured horseman uses both hands on his long cavalry spear, perhaps a *kontos* or *xyston*. The two Germanic warriors are probably Lombards, but are armed with swords and use round shields. Vandal heavy cavalry probably carried a single-handed spear and shield and heavily armoured Roman cavalry probably had a shield attached to the left arm; such units are still designated by a shield design in the *Notitia Dignitatum*. (Sailko/ Wikimedia/CC BY-SA 4.0)

to him (3.17.11). Gibamundus, however, nephew of Gelimer and present at Ad Decimum, seems to have been assigned men by Gelimer himself (3.18.1). When Gelimer seized the Vandal throne in 530, he not only imprisoned Hilderic but also his commander Hoamer and Hoamer's brother Euagees. This implies that loyalty to the commander or even the branch of the family in power was important and that Gelimer quickly replaced such men with male relatives of his own. Under Gelimer, armies were commanded by his brothers Tzazon and Ammatas and nephew Gibamundus (we do not know whose son he was, probably Ammatas'). Any residual loyalty to the previous regime can be discerned in the number of men who sought sanctuary after Gelimer's defeats and who were well treated by Belisarius.

Hughes (2009: 81) considers that the Vandals were different from their Roman counterparts because, whereas the Romans had an army into which men were recruited or who volunteered for service, the Vandals still operated on a tribal system in which every able-bodied warrior served in the army when necessary. Perhaps as a result of this tribal system, there seems to have been no regimented training regime for Vandal warriors other than hunting and other traditional pursuits, which may have taught skill in riding and with sword and spear. That said, there are clearly manoeuvres attempted by the Vandals, although they may not have been precise.

At some point the Alans, who had invaded the Roman Empire with other Gothic tribes in the 4th century, joined with the Vandals for their advance into Spain and the conquest of North Africa. They may have been primarily heavy cavalry. The title of King of the Vandals and Alans was adopted by Huneric only 50 years before, in the 480s. In the 530s the Alans were still present, but the sources refer to both groups under the single title of 'Vandals' even though we have archaeological evidence that Gelimer still used the title 'King of the Vandals and Alans'.

It seems probable that the Vandal armies consisted entirely of cavalry. Procopius never refers to the infantry of the Vandals like he does for the Roman forces arrayed against them. He tells us that in a battle against the Berbers:

> since the phalanx of the Moors was of such a sort, the Vandals were at a loss how to handle the situation; for they were neither good with the javelin nor with the bow, nor did they know how to go into battle on foot, but they were all horsemen, and used spears and swords for the most part, so that they were unable to do the enemy any harm at a distance; and their horses. (Procopius, *History of the Wars* 3.8.27)

This is a remarkable observation and one we might be reluctant to take at face value, especially if Procopius' numbers are accurate. Certainly, the Vandal flight and escape from pursuing Roman cavalry suggests they were all mounted. Vegetius certainly admired the horsemanship of the Alans

This artefact featuring a heavy cavalryman named Tryphon, found in Tanais (near modern-day Rostov-on-Don, Russia), possibly depicts an Alan heavy cavalryman. Vegetius (*De Re Militari* 3.26) tells us of the influence of their horsemanship on the Romans and they probably continued to serve in this way in Vandal armies, perhaps providing the heaviest cavalry – unlike the Vandals, who continued to use shield and spear. (Altes/Wikimedia/CC BY-SA 4.0)

(*De Re Militari* 3.26). Ammatas' contingent may have arrived piecemeal at Ad Decimum (Procopius 3.18.4–10) because some of his (mounted) troops were slower, perhaps because they were more heavily armoured than others or took longer to get organized, although the varying speeds of mounted and unmounted troops can also offer an explanation. Hughes (2009: 83) posits that the available evidence suggests the Vandals may indeed have adapted their army to be an all-cavalry force. Bury (1889: 128) also thought that the Vandal army consisted entirely of mounted troops wearing inferior armour, fighting with only the lance and the sword, being unskilled, in contrast to other Germanic peoples, in archery and the use of the javelin. In favour of such an interpretation, the Vandals had faced Berber and Saharan Bedouin enemies who were highly mobile, so it is possible – the loss of the horses before the battle of Ad Decimum is lamented (3.25.15) but might suggest some of the Vandal army had to go without mounts.

In his account of the Vandals in North Africa, Procopius tells us (3.5.18) they and their allies the Alans had 80,000 men organized into 80 companies, each commanded by a *chiliarch* (literally meaning commander of 1,000 – pl. *chiliarchoi*). The terms *chiliarch* and *chiliarchy* were, and had always been, military terms. This number of warriors had grown from 50,000 (3.5.19) in the previous century, indicating that the Vandals and Alans had clearly flourished. Procopius, when he wrote about the Vandals in the *Anecdota* (18.6), spoke of them as having eight myriads ('myriad' being the term for 10,000), so his count is consistent. Hughes (2009: 81–82) rejects 80,000 men as a standing military, however, and estimates only about 25,000 warriors as a military strength based on 80,000 as the total Vandal population. This would make Belisarius' apparently massively outnumbered force actually less so, although Hughes gives Belisarius 20,000 men, not the 15,000 (10,000 infantry and 5,000 cavalry) explicitly mentioned by Procopius. Belisarius'

This Vandal warrior from Carthage, commanded by Gelimer's brother Ammatas, prepares to meet the charge of a small force of heavy cavalry acting as Belisarius' advance guard. Confident in the plan to trap Belisarius' army between three prongs (Ammatas' blocking force, Gibamundus' flanking force to the west and Gelimer's main body), and in their superior numbers, the warrior is not to know that he and the remainder of Ammatas' forces will be routed by the small advance guard. Unlike the heavy *cataphractarii* that charge against him, the Vandal is lightly armed and armoured. The glory days of the Vandal conquest of North Africa are almost a century in the past and, although he is a proud descendant of those warriors, that heritage has been lost and perhaps squandered through soft living.

Weapons, dress and equipment

We are told that Vandals fought in all-cavalry armies but were not equipped with missile weapons. This warrior's primary armament is a heavy thrusting spear (**1**); he also carries a *spatha*, worn on his left hip. On his head is a looted *spangenhelm* (**2**) and he wears a long moustache in typical Vandal style. Unarmoured, he is clad in a long, decorated tunic (**3**), leggings (**4**) and shoes (**5**) typical of the period. He wears a round shield (**6**) on his left arm. He rides a horse descended from those which marched victoriously across France and Spain into North Africa a century earlier.

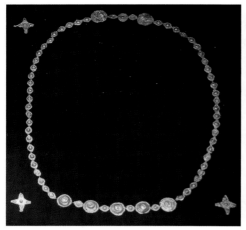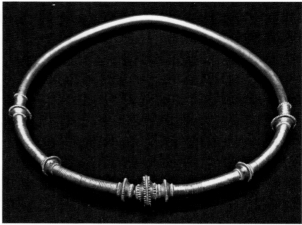

advancing confidently with only 15,000 men against such odds is difficult to accept and many scholars have lowered the number of actual warriors he faced. Bury (1889: 128) thought the Vandals had 30,000 men, Diehl (1896: 9) fewer than 40,000.

Hughes' suggestion that the 80,000 figure may have reflected the total Vandal population rejects Procopius' clear comment (*Anecdota* 18.6) that the number of women and children were incalculable and were in addition to the 80,000 warriors. For Hughes (2009: 82), the 1,000-man *chiliarchy* figure referred to 1,000 people and he estimates that each group of 1,000 supported a unit of only 300 warriors, giving a total of 24,000 men. When personal retinues are added this rises to his 25,000 estimate. This seems too low a figure, however, but it may be significant that the Vandal units subsequently recruited into the Roman cavalry were probably each 400 strong; if we accept Hughes' idea of lower numbers this may make a plausible contingent size. Assuming that 300 of each 1,000 people were warriors leaves 700 per 1,000 to represent the women, children and elderly – but this is probably too high a proportion. A more likely balance would be 400 warriors and 600 women, children and elderly; and we should remember that Vandal men probably began to ride as warriors at a young age and continued to fight well into old age.

MacDowall (2016: 122) argues for only 20,000 warriors in Vandal armies; the 80,000 population could, he argues, support 20,000 warriors (2016: 73), but later (2016: 129) he posits there may have been 30,000 warriors. In both MacDowall's and Hughes' lower estimates for the numbers of Vandals, the foolhardiness of Belisarius happily advancing against a force numbering more than four times his own is eliminated – their suggestions do, however, require the rejection of one set of Procopius' numbers while accepting others. If the 400-strong Vandal cavalry units subsequently serving in Byzantine armies accord with the size of such units when in Vandal service, the numbers provided are slightly larger than the 20,000 or 25,000 men of MacDowall and Hughes – 80 units of 400, giving us a total of 32,000 men. The figure of 32,000 (still much less than Procopius' 80,000) better preserves the idea of Belisarius' accomplishment, fighting at odds of more than two to one.

ORGANIZATION AND COMMAND

Byzantine

Procopius tells us that Belisarius was appointed commander 'with supreme authority over all' (*strategon de autokratora*; 3.11.18) and that 'the emperor gave him written instructions, bidding him do everything as seemed best to him, and stating that his acts would be final, as if the emperor himself had done them. The writing, in fact, gave him the power of a king' (3.11.20). The *strategon de autokratora* title may be Procopius' version of the Latin *comes et magister utriusque militiae* (supreme military commander), although he does not use that term.

Despite some remarkable details and insights, Procopius often reveals that he did not have detailed or professional knowledge of the workings of the contemporary Byzantine Army. He calls the *vexillum praetorium*, the standard, a *bandon*, which is an approximation of the Latin term *pannum* (4.2.1); elsewhere (4.10.4) he calls the man who held the *bandon* a 'bandifier' (*bandophoron* in Greek). He also, as we have noted, uses the term *doryphoroi* ('bodyguards', sing. *doryphoros*) in many places for Belisarius' *bucellarii*. What is more, he uses words such as *phalanx* (3.8.27, 3.23.12), probably in the general sense of a mass of men, although most military historians use it as a technical term. Elsewhere, however, Procopius can use an (unexpected) technical term, which seems entirely appropriate. For instance, he states 'Solomon commanded Theodorus, who led the *excubitores* (for thus the Romans call their guards) to take with him a thousand infantrymen' (4.12.17). The *excubitores* were, however, a 300-strong unit of imperial guards at Constantinople, created by the Eastern Roman Emperor Leo I (r. 457–74); Belisarius was himself appointed their commander in 550, a high honour (Procopius, *History of the Wars* 8.21.1). The *excubitores* should not, therefore, have been with Solomon in North Africa; neither did they number so many men. It is possible that Solomon was granted use of some imperial troops by Justinian I and that Procopius calls them *excubitores*. Prior to that there had been the *scholae palatinae* (guard units) at Constantinople, composed of seven 500-strong units of heavy cavalry. The

status of these units had deteriorated over time, however, and they no longer saw active service, something Agathias laments (*Histories* 5.15.1–6); he tells us this period of decline began under the Eastern Roman Emperor Zeno I (r. 474–91). Procopius probably means Solomon's *bucellarii*, but it is odd that he uses the wrong designation for them, which might suggest they were supplied by the emperor rather than raised by Solomon himself.

An exactly contemporary edict from Justinian I, issued on 13 April 534 to Belisarius in North Africa (*Codex Justinianus* 1.27.2:19–36), usefully gives us the pay grades (if not actual ranks) in the 6th-century Byzantine Army. An unexpected corroboration of much of the list comes from Jerome (*To Pammachius Against John of Jerusalem* 19). These two sources tell us of the ranks (in descending order), and it seems that such ranks were the same in infantry and cavalry formations. The *ducenarius* was commander of two centuries, the *centenaries* was commander of a century and the *biarchus* was possibly the commander of a *contubernium* or tent group (other terms for this rank included *caput contubernii* and *decanus*). The *biarchus* was a double-pay man, another term for which was *duplicarius*. Another double-pay position was the *circitor*, possibly someone entrusted with sentry duty. Below this were *semissales* (sing. *semissalis*) earning one-and-a-half times pay, equivalent to a junior NCO. Jerome provides the ranks below this of standard recruits – *pedes* (infantry) or *eques* (cavalry) – and of the new recruit, or *tiro*. These two sources show that the systems remained the same as in the time of Jerome (writing in the late 4th century) and an edict of 534. Some ranks above these are listed, including the *dux* (usually commander of a province), *adsessor* (judicial adviser to the *dux*), *primicerius* (chief clerk) and *numerarius* (chief accountant), although these may be civil offices. Jerome's letter (*To Pammachius Against John of Jerusalem* 19) names *tribunus* (tribune), then *primicerius* and *senator* before *ducenarius*. Even though Procopius only gives us the names of commanders (and omits their rank), we can use lists like these to build a picture of how the command structure of Belisarius' army looked.

Vandal

In many aspects of military culture, the Vandals were probably very similar to the armies of Belisarius they faced. The cavalry of the Vandals could be incorporated into Byzantine armies immediately following Belisarius' triumph (Procopius 4.14.17). So too could Cyril be sent to Sardinia to reinforce Godas (Procopius 3.11.1–2) without there being any concern as to how the forces would cooperate. Moreover, when the mutiny occurred under Stotzas, he could relatively easily invite the 1,000 mutinying Vandals to join him and incorporate them into his forces (4.15.2–4). All this suggests that there was probably a similarity between the armament, language and perhaps tactics employed by Vandal armies and those used by their Byzantine adversaries. The Byzantine Army of the 6th century might also have allowed for any variations in tactics (such as those used by the Huns and other contingents of *foederati*) to be incorporated and might have given such units sufficient space and opportunity in which to employ them, such as the Huns operating separately at the battle of Ad Decimum (3.18.12–18) and standing apart at the battle of Tricamarum (4.3.5). That

This mosaic from Bordj Djedid near Carthage, Tunisia, shows a Vandal horseman and dates from the late 5th or early 6th centuries. The details show that Vandal dress differed very little from Roman – decorated, long-sleeved, short tunics with leggings and cloak. The man is probably an aristocrat and his long hair and moustache mark him out as a Vandal. The horse trappings, however, may reveal slight differences in how Vandal horses were fitted out. (Print Collector/Getty Images)

being said, the Vandals who invaded the Roman Empire in 406 may not have been influenced by Roman practices and their successes would have given them very little reason to change their approach. What is more, once they crossed into North Africa in 429 and met with even greater success into the 450s, their relative isolation might have hindered the incorporation of Byzantine military practices. Conversely, the Vandals' successes could have influenced aspects of Byzantine organization, as hinted at by Vegetius (*De Re Militari* 1.20, 3.26).

We are provided with the names of the commanders of large contingents or Vandal armies – such as Tzazon's 5,000 men sent with him to Sardinia (Procopius 3.11.23), or the forces of Ammatas, Gibamundus' 2,000 cavalry (3.18.1) and Gelimer's command. Below that, however, we are not given much detail.

In his account of the battle of Tricamarum (3.18.1), Procopius again writes of the Vandal *chiliarchoi*, although he states that each one commanded a division (4.3.8), for which he uses the term *lochoi* (sing. *lochos*) – a generic Greek term, although rare in Procopius; it is also used to describe 'companies' (3.5.18). Procopius also speaks of a *keras* ('wing') of the Vandal army (4.3.8).

Another Vandal horseman mosaic from Bordj Djedid near Carthage. Although a hunting scene, the horse trappings depicted will have been the same as for their military operations. Other hunting mosaics show that weapons (even swords and shields) were used on hunting expeditions. This man uses a lasso – something we have attested for the cavalry forces of the Huns who 'entangled their enemies with twisted cords' (*contortis laciniis iligant*. Ammianus, 31.2.9). Vegetius (*De Re Militari* 3.23.2) also mentions lassos (using the term *laquei*) as being a weapon to which *cataphractarii* were vulnerable. It is possible that lassos were used by the Vandals in battle, especially against heavily armoured *bucellarii*. The Parthians also used lassos (*Suda* Σ 278). Procopius singles these men out for praise as 'men endowed with bravery and endurance in the highest degree' (3.11.11). (Print Collector/Getty Images)

These terms either had specific meanings earlier in military history or acquired them subsequently, but Procopius seems to use them in a general sense. It is not clear (but seems unlikely) that the Vandals used terms like *lochos* for their 'divisions' or 'companies'. Most common in Procopius, however, is the term *katalogos*, usually reserved for a list or register of soldiers in a unit but used uniquely by Procopius to refer to a group of soldiers (3.11.5, 3.11.18, 3.14.14, 4.3.4, 4.10.5, 4.14.17, 4.14.18 & 4.15.20). Procopius uses this term where we would expect *arithmos*, but it probably reflects his role as Belisarius' *assessor* (legal secretary) and is perhaps a classicizing reference to the *katalogos* of ancient Athens (Whately 2021: 58, 84). Procopius does not use the term *tagma*, which became standard later in the century.

Despite the idea that such men were equipped and armed largely uniformly, it would seem that the Vandals did not use the same hierarchy of officers as Byzantine armies did. Procopius gives us the detail of 80 *chiliarchoi*, each one commanding 1,000 men (3.5.18, reiterated at *Anecdota* 18.6); this may be an accurate detail or an approximation of the officers (the term is an old-fashioned Greek one). Hughes considers (2009: 81) that this was the equivalent of an actual Germanic title, *thusundifath*, also meaning commander of 1,000; the command of 1,000 was a common one among ancient armies. It may be that the tribal affiliations which made up the peoples of the Vandals and the Goths were each considered to number approximately 1,000 men, although Hughes argues (2009: 82) that each *thusundifath* actually commanded only 300 men.

Hughes suggests (2009: 82) that the Vandals' other officers – such as decurions and centurions – may have reflected Roman systems. There is no evidence of this and, if the contingent size of 400 is correct, smaller increments and officers may not have been necessary. A unit size of 1,000 men would seem to be unwieldy, but we do not know of any junior officer-type designations.

TACTICS AND EQUIPMENT

Byzantine

At the beginning of his account of the Persian Wars, which began in the late 520s and involved largely the same army Belisarius would take to North Africa, Procopius provides a remarkable summary of the state of the Byzantine Army:

> There are those, for example, who call the soldiers of the present day 'bowmen' (*toxotas*), while to those of the most ancient times they wish to attribute such lofty terms as 'hand-to-hand fighters' (*agchemachos*), 'shield-men' (*aspidiotas*), and other names of that sort; and they think that the valour of those times has by no means survived to the present – an opinion which is at once careless and wholly remote from actual experience of these matters. (Procopius, *History of the Wars* 1.1.8–17)

This accords with the idea that nearly all contemporary Byzantine soldiers were bowmen, but they also had shields, armour and horse armour, unlike the archers of earlier eras. Procopius also makes reference (1.1.11) to developments

These two hunters from a 6th-century mosaic at the Great Palace, Constantinople, wield their spears two-handed (against a tiger), using a technique shown in use more often by cavalry. Their colourful tunics and leggings help suggest just how vibrant the colours of everyday clothes could be; and this and other evidence suggests that armies of the day could have been a riot of colour both in tunic and shield designs. (ullstein bild/Getty Images)

Dating from the reign of Justinian I, this mosaic from the Great Palace in Constantinople depicts a hunter using a shield and spear and shows the off-centre shield grip. Cavalry shields seem to have been of a very similar design. (funkyfood London - Paul Williams/Alamy Stock Photo)

in bow technology (Homeric archers only drawing their bow to the chest) and contends that:

> the bowmen of the present time go into battle wearing corselets and fitted out with greaves which extend up to the knee. From the right side hang their arrows, from the other the sword. And there are some who have a spear also attached to them and, at the shoulders, a sort of small shield without a grip, such as to cover the region of the face and neck. They are expert horsemen, and are able without difficulty to direct their bows to either side while riding at full speed, and to shoot an opponent whether in pursuit or in flight. They draw the bowstring along by the forehead about opposite the right ear, thereby charging the arrow with such an impetus as to kill whoever stands in the way, shield and corselet alike having no power to check its force. (Procopius, *History of the Wars* 1.1.12–14)

This seems to suggest that all cavalry were indeed capable of performing as archers and even perhaps that infantry rode to battle. Procopius does tell us (3.11.11) that all of the Huns were bowmen. By the time of the Byzantine Emperor Maurice (r. 582–602), only a few decades later, the idea that all soldiers were archers was cemented – the opening line of his *Strategikon* (1.1) states that all men should practise archery on foot and mounted. It is also clear that the two methods of drawing the bowstring were learned from the Huns (although called the Roman method) or the Persians. Vegetius (*De Re Militari* 1.20) tells us that the Romans improved their archery in the late 4th or early 5th centuries by copying the techniques of the Huns, Goths and Alans. Procopius also makes reference to the use of spears (3.19.13, 3.23.14–16 & 4.2.6).

This 6th- or 7th-century tunic from Egypt shows an item of clothing that was ubiquitous across the area formerly encompassed by the Roman Empire and worn by both Byzantine and Vandal. The intricate decoration we see here is often rendered as lines on mosaics and in other art forms, but the patterns could be individual and highly complex. (Knop92/Wikimedia/Public Domain)

The Infantry Treatise 'B' in Maurice's *Strategikon* (12B.1–24), written during the reign of Justinian I, begins with an index describing the 24 chapters of the treatise that deal with training, arms, armament and clothing, as well as formations and organization. The short preface states that the pamphlet was written for officers to put into practice. As well as being fascinating for the army of Justinian I in general, it has several pertinent points for the cavalry of the Vandalic War. In chapter 6, wagons pulled by pack horses are recommended, one for each *dekarchy* (squad), for carrying all manner of essential tools. This corresponds to the wagons used to shore up the line at the battle of Scalae Veteres (Procopius 4.17.4). The treatise postulates that cavalry should be deployed outside the infantry (*Strategikon* 12B.12) and, in the battles in which infantry were used in coordination with cavalry by Belisarius and Germanus, this was indeed done. The depth of cavalry is recommended as ten ranks deep if the army is large with 12,000 cavalry, otherwise a depth of five ranks is recommended. We may therefore suggest that Belisarius drew up his 5,000 cavalry five ranks deep. Reckless pursuit of fleeing enemies was discouraged, and may have been something Belisarius tried to trick the Vandals into doing at the battle of Tricamarum. The battle of Ad Decimum is the perfect illustration of chapter 19 – marching if the enemy is nearby. It is recommended that cavalry patrols should be sent out front and rear: Belisarius used both. Entrenchments and the guarding of camps is recommended, and we are told of Belisarius also taking this precaution regularly (Procopius 3.15.29, 3.15.36, 3.17.7 & 3.19.1).

Vandal

It is clear from the Vandal-era mosaics of North Africa that their dress, arms and armour were very similar to those of the men they faced. Such forces had operated as *foederati* in Roman armies and so equipment too was similar. Procopius mentions Gelimer instructing his forces to fight only with the sword before the battle of Tricamarum and not with a spear or 'any other weapon' (4.3.9). This suggests that, like the contemporary Roman armies, the Vandal forces used a variety of weapons, even including lassos.

This decorated fragment of a 6th-century tunic from Egypt (now in the Cleveland Museum of Art, Inv. 1914.531) shows how intricate such designs could be on even the plainest garments. (Gift of J.H. Wade/Cleveland Museum of Art/Wikimedia/ CC0 1.0)

The Alans, closely associated with the Vandals for more than two centuries, were renowned for their cavalry forces and had fought at the battle of Adrianople in 378 as cavalry (Ammianus 31.2–3, 31.12.17), and it is unlikely those tactics had changed. When used as *foederati*, they would have been encouraged to use the tactics to which they were accustomed. Although the Alans are usually depicted as spear-armed heavy cavalry, they may also have operated as horse-archers, perhaps performing both roles. Vegetius (*De Re Militari* 1.20) recognized that the archery of the Goths, Alans and Huns had taught the Romans a thing or two. This also suggests that the Alans may have provided archery for the Vandals, a skill the Vandals themselves lacked according to Procopius (3.8.27). In Procopius' writings, however, Alan archery is never mentioned.

We are uninformed as to how the Vandals operated in battle; they may have mirrored Roman formations and Procopius does describe them operating in left, right and central divisions, just like the Roman armies they fought. This may, however, be a literary tradition. Procopius tells us (4.3.8) that at Tricamarum, Tzazon's division was in the centre and either wing was made up of the forces of other Vandal *chiliarchoi*, each one leading a *lochos*. In the final battle of the mutineers at Scalae Veteres in 536, however, Stotzas arrayed his men in a single block, 'more in the manner of barbarians' (4.17.7), which might reflect actual Vandal practice. We can note once more that the Vandals in Stotzas' army were easily included and incorporated into such a deployment. Despite this instance, it is clear that the Vandals were also capable of complex manoeuvres. The entire Vandal plan for the battle of Ad Decimum, despite it coming undone and ending in utter defeat, was a sound one that involved a three-pronged surrounding of Belisarius' exposed and vulnerable marching

A 6th- or 7th-century pair of leather shoes from Egypt; they accord with the popular designs we see in mosaics and other art. Even soldiers seem to have worn shoes or cross-laced boots rather than any kind of military footwear as was common in centuries past. These shoes are incised with designs so were probably owned by someone relatively wealthy. (Sepia Times/Getty Images)

army (3.17.11). Moreover, it is clear that Belisarius took great pains to protect his march from just such a tactic being used against him. Even Procopius all but admits the Vandals should not have lost (3.18.3, 3.19.25). Likewise, at the battle of the Bagradas River, the mutineers and Vandals attempted what was a rather complex redeployment of their entire force to one wing (4.15.43). The fact that this was undone by an (unexpected) frontal charge from Belisarius' cavalry does not undermine the finesse and training needed to undertake such manoeuvres even though it was noted that it was carried out in some disorder. At the same time, however, Procopius mentions the contempt Belisarius had for Stotzas' forces being without generals (4.15.15). By the time of the final battle at Scalae Veteres, however, Stotzas may not have expected his mutinying forces to operate with the training and practice necessary to deploy in such a way – or that when they had, it had resulted in defeat – so he arranged them in a single mass: one which had some success against the Byzantine infantry until the actions of Germanus' charge forced the Vandals and mutineers to flee (4.17.18).

Based on the available archaeological record, Vandal warriors seem to have favoured simple *spangenhelm* (segmented helmet) designs and to have continued to use mail and scale armour, although they may have worn less armour than their Byzantine opponents. Much of this armour may have been looted from their journey across Gaul, Spain and North Africa (not to mention from Italy and Rome in the 450s). There is no evidence for the use of greaves or vambraces, however, and Vandals retained their use of large, round shields. All were armed with long swords and spears and there is evidence of their knowledge and experience of how to use lassos. When Gelimer commanded his men to attack with swords only (4.3.9), the expectation was that every warrior had one. Hughes observes (2009: 83) that the Vandals did not use spears as missile weapons, but kept them for thrusting in hand-to-hand combat. The Vandals also seem to have had little in the way of missile troops, certainly in the way they are described – perhaps reflected in the very low casualties suffered by the Romans.

Ad Decimum

15 September AD 533

BACKGROUND TO BATTLE

In June 533, Justinian I sent Belisarius (in company with his wife Antonia) to North Africa; the expedition left Constantinople around the time of the summer solstice (*amphi therinas tropas*; 22 June), in the seventh year of Justinian I's reign (Procopius 3.12.1): 'there was with them also Procopius, who wrote this history' (3.12.3).

The fleet put in at Heracleia (or Neapolis, near modern-day Eriklice Köyü, Turkey), taking on 'an exceedingly great number of horses' (Procopius 3.12.6), a gift from Justinian I. The fleet sailed on to Abydos (on the Nara Burnu or Cape Nara, Nagara Point in the Dardanelles, near the modern-day city of Çanakkale, Turkey) (3.12.7). There, Procopius recounts an anecdote which is highly informative for Belisarius' style of leadership; two of his Hun allies killed one of their colleagues in a drunken argument. Belisarius immediately impaled the two perpetrators, displaying their bodies on a prominent hill. The families of the men accused him of acting beyond the terms of their agreement (3.12.8–10). It seems peculiar to us that both Belisarius and his men travelled on this campaign with their families, but this seems to have been the practice. Belisarius also spoke of the justice of their cause (3.12.21). We can see the positive effects of such a policy later when Procopius confirms that the army was well behaved on the march towards Carthage (3.17.6).

The fleet left Abydos and continued to Sigeum (or Sigeon, modern-day Kumkale, Çanakkale Province, Turkey), then to Malea (which could be the modern-day town of Akhlia or Cape Agrilia, the south-easternmost point of Lesbos, Greece), then Taenarum (modern-day Cape Matapan, Greece). At Methone (modern-day Methoni, Greece) on the easternmost tip of the Peloponnese, Belisarius found Valerian and Martinus waiting with their

This silver *denarius* of Gelimer (the legend 'Gilamir' can clearly be made out) obviously copies Roman types even though the *denarius* had been superseded in Constantinople. Minted in Carthage, the coins adopted the use of 'DN' – *Dominus Noster* ('Our Lord') – the same Latin title used for Roman legends. The letter under the 'DN' is 'L', representing 50, although Gelimer's reign only lasted three years. (Historic Images/ Alamy Stock Photo)

Discovered at Dougga (or Thugga), Tunisia, and now held in the Museé National Du Bardo in Tunis, this 3rd- or 4th-century mosaic of Ulysses shows boat designs that reflect the kinds Belisarius would have used. (Ulysses' men are depicted in contemporary fashion with round shields.) The fleet required to transport Belisarius' expedition amounted to 500 ships, each of which had a capacity of 3,000 *medimni* or more (a *medimnos* was a measure of volume ranging between 50 and 70 litres), one of the ships having a capacity of 50,000 *medimni* (2.5–3.5 million litres) (Procopius 3.11.13). This fleet was manned by 30,000 sailors from Egypt, Ionia and Cilicia; Calonymus of Alexandria was appointed as the *archegos* (commander) of the fleet (3.11.14). Among the ships were 92 'ships prepared as for sea-fighting' (3.11.15), with a single bank of oars and covered decks. Such fast ships were called 'dromones' (*dromonas* in Greek, meaning 'runners'), manned by 2,000 rowers from Constantinople who also fought as needed; 'there was not a single superfluous man among them' (3.11.16). In addition to Calonymus, Archelaus, the *praefectus* (prefect) of the army, was also sent to maintain the army (3.11.17). MacDowall points out (2016: 122) that Belisarius' fleet was less than half the size of those involved in the failed Roman and Byzantine invasions of Vandal North Africa in 441, 460 and 468, which had 1,100 ships. Archaeological Museum, Tunis, Tunisia (Inv. 2884A). (Jerzystrzelecki/Wikimedia/ CC BY 3.0)

contingents to join the expedition (3.13.9); these had been sent on in advance from Constantinople (3.9.24). At Methone, Belisarius disembarked the whole army and held a review: 'he assigned the commanders their positions and drew up the soldiers' (3.13.10). In this way he seems to have prepared the men for the march in battle formation that he would undertake as soon as he landed in North Africa.

From Methone, the fleet sailed to Zacynthus (modern-day Zacynthos, or Zante, on the island of Zakynthos, Greece) and then on to the coast of Sicily, which took 16 days (3.13.21–23). There they discovered that the water had spoiled (3.13.23). According to Procopius, Belisarius sent him ahead to Syracuse to discover if there were Vandal ships lying in ambush and to discover a good anchorage for the fleet in Libya (3.14.1–3). Procopius may have exaggerated (or invented) this mission because he was also sent to buy provisions (3.14.5). Procopius learned that there would be no Vandal naval ambush and, in fact, the Vandals had no idea an expedition was coming against them (3.14.7–9). Gelimer was in the city of Hermione in Byzacena (the city's location is unknown although Capsa – modern-day Gafsa, Tunisia – is the best candidate). This was four days' journey (157km) from the coast (3.14.10). Others may have provided local intelligence too; Zacharias Rhetor (*Ecclesiastical History* 9.17) refers to African nobles who had fled to Justinian I at Constantinople.

Belisarius learned that Dorotheus, commander of the *foederati* from Armenia, had died (3.14.14) but 'issued orders to give the signal for departure' (3.14.15). The fleet stopped briefly at the islands of Gaulus and Melita (modern-day Gozo and Malta) and then proceeded to Libya (3.14.17). They landed (probably in early September) at a place Procopius calls 'Shoal's Head' (*Kephalen Brachous*), derived from its name 'Caputvada' (*Karchedonos* in Greek), 'five days' journey from Carthage for an unencumbered traveller' (3.14.17). This exact location has vexed scholars although it falls within only a narrow band of possibilities and is probably Cape Vada (modern-day Ras Kaboudia, Tunisia) and the (modern-day) town of Chebba. From their camp, made as soon as they disembarked, the city of Syllectus (modern-day Salakta, Tunisia) was one day's march (3.16.9).

Procopius recounts an argument about plans for disembarkation (3.15.2–17). Archelaus, the *praefectus* (prefect) of the army, suggested that the journey would take nine days without water and that they should, instead, sail straight to Carthage. At 40km per day, the 258km journey from Cape Vada to Carthage would take longer than this, but it is probable that these distances were not exact

The oasis town of Capsa (modern-day Gafsa, Tunisia) is a good candidate for Hermione, where Gelimer learned of Belisarius' landing, perhaps being surprised at the Byzantines coming. From this location, it is possible to see why Gelimer's Vandals pursued the Byzantine forces making their way up the coast. The city would go on to be the capital of Byzacena under Byzantine control. (Habib M'henni/Wikimedia/ CC BY-SA 3.0)

– slightly more than 50km per day can fit Procopius' five-day march figure.

Procopius' argument is highly unlikely, however, and the plan for disembarkation had probably been in place for some time. Indeed, Belisarius' plan (3.15.18–30) was adopted: 'I say that we must disembark upon the land with all possible speed, landing horses and arms and whatever else we consider necessary for our use, and that we must dig a trench quickly and throw a stockade around us of a kind which can contribute to our safety no less than any walled town one might mention, and with that as our base must carry on the war from there if anyone should attack us' (3.15.29). This was probably the only plan there had been all along.

The journey from Constantinople to disembarkation took about three months (3.15.31), not the 140 days John the Cappadocian estimated it would take when he opposed the enterprise (3.10.14). The army disembarked and encamped, even finding a water spring, something unexpected in a waterless land (3.15.34).

Belisarius instructed one of his commanders, Boriades, to take some guard cavalry and attempt to take the city of Syllectus, the walls of which had been torn down. The city was taken with ease the following morning (3.16.9–11) and a large number of horses were captured along with the deserting Vandal overseer (3.16.12). A postal courier was also captured who was then given a letter from Justinian I to give to the Vandals proclaiming that he was attempting to dethrone a tyrant and maintain peace with the Vandal people and their rightful king (3.16.13–14). Unfortunately, the courier did not dare to reveal this letter publicly, such was the fear of Gelimer and his brother Ammatas, so it did not achieve its aim of removing the Vandals from their loyalty to Gelimer. Belisarius then marched his army to Syllectus.

The location of the remarkably well-preserved ruins of Sufetula (modern-day Subeitla, Tunisia), another candidate for Hermione. Its location probably meant that Gelimer could get ahead of Belisarius' march (especially if his army consisted entirely of cavalry) and arrive at Carthage ahead of the Byzantines. The unspoiled nature of the remains is also a testament to the occasional lack of destruction under the Vandals. (Dennis Jarvis/ Wikimedia/CC BY-SA 2.0)

1 Belisarius marches in battle formation. A force of 300 *bucellarii* cavalry commanded by John (**A**) act as a vanguard some 4km ahead of the main body. The 600 Hun cavalry (**B**) operate as a flank guard to the west of the advancing army. The remainder of the Byzantine army (**C**), with Belisarius in the rear, marches towards Ad Decimum, making camp some 7km from Ad Decimum.

2 Ammatas (**D**) proceeds from Carthage but his forces are disorganized. Gibamundus (**E**) has been sent with 2,000 cavalry to approach Ad Decimum from the west. Gelimer, meanwhile, with the remaining Vandal force (**F**), has taken a more inland route to Ad Decimum (perhaps branching off at modern-day Grombalia, Tunisia) and has overtaken Belisarius' main army.

3 Ammatas reaches Ad Decimum too early, arriving at midday. John's heavy cavalry charge Ammatas' ill-prepared but probably numerically superior force. John's 300 *bucellarii* cavalry suffer 12 casualties but rout the Vandal cavalry, killing Ammatas. The Byzantine cavalry pursue the fleeing Vandals and, coming across small groups making their way to the battlefield, slay many in their pursuit, which reaches the walls of Carthage itself.

4 Gibamundus' force of 2,000 Vandal cavalry reaches the salt plain, Pedion Halon, some 8.5km west of Ad Decimum. The 600 Huns of Belisarius' flank guard encounter Gibamundus' force and immediately charge. The Vandals, with no missile troops, cannot withstand the mounted archers

of the Huns. Gibamundus is killed and the Huns pursue the fleeing Vandals.

5 Leaving his infantry in camp, Belisarius advances with his remaining cavalry (some 4,100 men). He sends his *foederati* commanders (Solomon, Cyprian, Valerian, Martinus, Althias, John the Armenian and Marcellus) forward in seven, roughly 400-man units, approximately 2,800 men. These reach the spot at Ad Decimum where Ammatas was killed.

6 Gelimer's main force approaches Ad Decimum. The *foederati* commanders send word to Belisarius to hurry. Gelimer charges the *foederati*, fighting for possession of the high ground thereabouts, and drives them off.

7 The *foederati* withdraw 1.5km to the south-east. There, they are met by Uliaris with 800 *bucellarii* sent forward by Belisarius. Rather than charge the Vandals, both units withdraw towards Belisarius.

8 Gelimer finds the body of his brother Ammatas and is distraught. He orders his men to prepare a burial. Belisarius meets the retiring cavalry and then advances with his combined cavalry force. The Byzantines arrive at Ad Decimum and charge the unprepared Vandals who have dispersed to prepare for Ammatas' burial. The Vandals break and flee. The Byzantines pursue until nightfall (around 1830hrs).

Battlefield environment

Despite Procopius telling us (3.17.11) that Ad Decimum was 70 *stadia* (12.9–14.7km) from Carthage and the name itself implying that it should be sought 10 Roman miles from the city, usually calculated at 80 *stadia* (14.8–16.9km), an exact pinpointing of the site has not been attempted in recent times – that site would, however, be in the middle of modern-day Tunis. Another reason for this lack of a pinpointed location is that the battle itself took place over several locations – Ad Decimum itself; Pedion Halon (meaning 'salt plain'), a location perhaps 8.5km to the west of Ad Decimum, where Gibamundus' force of 2,000 was destroyed by the Hun *foederati*; and the road back to Carthage, where John's 300 *bucellarii* pursued Ammatas' fleeing forces.

The location of Pedion Halon would still be within the suburbs of modern-day Tunis (perhaps around Manouba or El Agba). The battle was also one of manoeuvre, as Belisarius had John's force out ahead of him, the Huns off to his left, and he was being pursued by Gelimer's forces, which were closer than he imagined and actually managed to get around him and reach Ad Decimum from the south before he could.

Tissot's exploration of the environs (Tissot 1888: 114–21) led him to consider that Belisarius' camp should be placed at Hammam el-Enf (modern-day Hammam Lif, Tunisia), on a rocky spur of the hill there at the northern end of the defile. Tissot placed the battlefield itself near the train station of Jebel Jeullud (modern-day Jebel Jeloud, Tunis), which was then outside the city's south-eastern gate (Bab Alleona). Behind hills close by to the west (Megrin and Sidi Fathalla) extended a salt plain (Sebkhaes-Sejuni). The scholar J.B. Bury noted that in recent times it was 'an arid and treeless tract then as now' (Bury 1889: 132). Bury envisaged the Vandal plan to be that Ammatas confronted Belisarius in the defile while Gibamundus crossed the salt plain to descend on the Roman left flank. Gelimer was to approach from the rear and trap them. Belisarius' Huns were, Bury estimates (1889: 133–34), heading for Sidi Fathalla (close to Jebel Jeloud) when they came across Gibamundus' force. Gelimer was proceeding overland on a more southerly route, perhaps from modern-day Grombalia, Tunisia, keeping west of the hills at Jebel Bu-Kornin (now the Boukornine National Park).

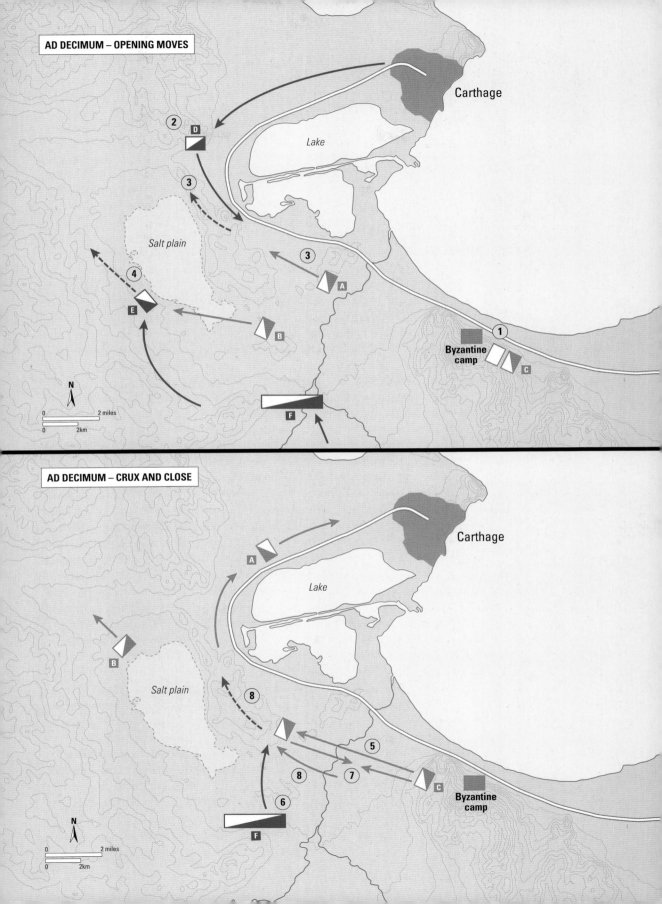

AD DECIMUM – OPENING MOVES

Carthage

Lake

② D

③

Salt plain

③ A

④

E

B

① Byzantine camp

C

F

N

0   2 miles
0   2km

AD DECIMUM – CRUX AND CLOSE

Carthage

Lake

A

Salt plain

B

⑧

⑤

⑧ ⑦

C

⑥

Byzantine camp

F

N

0   2 miles
0   2km

This silver *denarius* minted at Carthage depicts Hilderic with a diadem on the obverse and the legend 'DNHILDERIXREX', signifying 'Our Lord Hilderic King'; on the reverse is a personification of the city of Carthage and the legend 'KARTGFELIX', 'Lucky Carthage'. (Historic Images/ Alamy Stock Photo)

INTO COMBAT

Procopius' account of the battle comes in his *History of the Wars* (3.17.1– 20.9). He begins by telling us (3.17.1–3) Belisarius' order of march, arrayed in battle order. The Byzantine general was clearly expecting to fight soon after his arrival. We can calculate the date of the battle as Procopius tells us (3.21.23–25) that the churches of Carthage were being decorated for the feast of St Cyprian to be celebrated the following day – St Cyprian's feast day was 16 September. Some reconstructions place the battle on the 13th. John, the man 'in charge of the expenditures of the general's household' (3.17.1), is identified by Procopius as being from Armenia, although he refers to him simply as 'John' to differentiate him from John the Armenian, one of the *foederati* commanders. Procopius gives John the old-fashioned rank of *optio*. John was put in charge of 300 *bucellarii* and commanded to move ahead of the main body of Belisarius' army by a distance of at least 20 stadia (3.7km using 185m per stade; 4.2km using Procopius' 211m per *stade*). This distance of 20 *stadia*, Belisarius considered, was sufficient that, if John did see anything, he could ride back rapidly and report, giving Belisarius' troops time to prepare. Belisarius commanded the 600 Hun cavalry to travel on the left flank of his army, keeping the same distance away as John's contingent. Belisarius himself marched at the rear of the column with his best troops.

According to Procopius, Belisarius suspected that Gelimer (who was following his forces from the city of Hermione) would attack the Byzantine force on the march. Belisarius' right flank was protected by the sea and he commanded that the ships should follow the army closely; if the wind was not favourable they should row to keep up (3.17.5).

Belisarius' forces reached Syllectus where his troops did not plunder or begin fights with the locals – part of a policy of winning the Libyan population over to his side. Continuing his march, he 'made the journey as if in his own land' (3.17.6). The locals did not hide at Belisarius' approach but advised him about the locale and held a market for the soldiers where they could obtain anything they needed. According to Procopius (3.17.7), the march to Carthage was accomplished with progress of 80 *stadia* (14.8–16.9km) per day. Procopius does not tell us how many days this took, but each night was spent in a city or a fortified camp. A day's travel (unencumbered) was usually estimated by Procopius (3.1.17) as 210 *stadia* (38.8–44.3km).

The march progressed to the city of Leptis (or Leptis Parva, modern-day Monastir, Tunisia), then Hadrumentum (now a suburb of the city of Sousse, Tunisia), and reached a place called Grasse, 350 *stadia* (64.8–73.8km) from Carthage. This was perhaps around Pupput (modern-day Hammamet, Tunisia), a name that means 'baths'; located 81km from Carthage, it was the site of Gelimer's garden palace. Tissot (1888: 116) located Grasse at Sidi-Khelifa, Tunisia, 35km south of Hammamet and location of the Roman archaeological site of Feradi Maius (or Pheradi Majius). The garden palace's orchards were bearing fruit, and Belisarius' army made camp among the trees and all ate their fill; Procopius states that 'there was practically no diminution to be seen' (3.17.10) in the fruit on the trees. This kind of detail reminds us of Procopius' presence with the expedition (not to mention corroborating a mid-September date for the campaign). Procopius thus gives us five camp names

The ruins of Syllectus (modern-day Salakta, Tunisia). Procopius tells us that the town was one day's march from the landing point of Belisarius' fleet. Using the (sometimes contradictory) information he gives us elsewhere (3.1.17, 3.17.1), we can calculate that the landing point was therefore at Cape Vada and the (modern-day) town of Chebba, 23km south of Salakta. (Rais67/ Wikimedia/Public Domain)

but, marching 14.8–16.9km each day, there must have been other stops on the march – to cover the distance to Ad Decimum would have entailed 14–16 days' marching. They must have made progress every day or else they landed on 1 September (the battle was fought on 15 September). For instance, the distance between Cape Vada and Salakta was 23km and could be managed in a longer-than-usual day's march. Marching that distance each day, the army would have reached Ad Decimum in only ten days (close to Archelaus' nine days), suggesting that the landing occurred on 5 September; Procopius' three months for the sea journey is therefore an overestimate; it was more like only 11 weeks. Gibbon (1788: 629) estimated 10–12 days' march.

At Hermione, when Gelimer learned of the Byzantine presence, he wrote to his brother Ammatas at Carthage, instructing him to kill Hilderic and any others with a claim to the throne Gelimer had usurped. He also ordered his brother to ready the forces in the city so that when Belisarius reached the narrow approach to the city 'which they call Decimum' (*Dekimon* in Greek) (3.17.11), the two brothers could attack Belisarius from both sides, surround him and catch him as if in a net, and destroy him.

Ammatas did as he was instructed and killed Hilderic and all his family and supporters. He then armed the Vandals and prepared to spring Gelimer's trap. Gelimer, meanwhile, did as Belisarius suspected he would, and set out from Hermione to shadow his march. He kept his pursuit secret until reaching Grasse, where his forward scouts ran into the Belisarius' rear scouts; the two sides exchanged blows before retiring to their respective camps. This contact, Procopius informs us (3.17.14), told the Byzantines that the Vandals were not far away. What is more, as the march progressed the next day, the ships could not be seen to the right of the army, as a projecting headland (probably Cape Bon) had caused them to make a detour (3.17.15); their absence caused consternation in the Byzantine ranks. Knowing that his fleet would need to make this detour, Belisarius advised its commanders, the prefect Archelaus and the *navarch* (admiral) Calonymus, not to put in at Carthage but to stay about 200 *stadia* (37–42.2km) away and await his instructions. The Byzantine army departed from Grasse and proceeded towards Ad Decimum.

The ruins of Pupput (modern-day Hammamet, Tunisia), 81km from Carthage. This might have been the site of Grasse and Gelimer's garden palace where Belisarius camped among the fruit orchards (3.17.10). Procopius gives us relatively precise details on the distances marched in Libya, which help us to identify potential locations, telling us that 'one day's journey extends two hundred and ten *stadia*' (3.1.17) – the distance between Athens and Megara (41.2km on modern roads). This is his unencumbered travelling distance, however, and the army marched slightly less than half of that in a day. Procopius tells us they marched 80 *stadia* per day (3.17.7), so between 14.8km and 16.9km. The distance from Belisarius' landing point at Cape Vada (modern-day Ras Kaboudia, Tunisia) to Salakta was 23km. A *stade* is usually taken to be about 185m, with eight *stadia* making up one Roman mile (1,480m). Procopius, however, places the battlefield of Ad Decimum, meaning 'at the tenth' (mile), 70 *stadia* from Carthage (3.17.11), so has only seven *stadia* per Roman mile, not the usual eight; this would make his *stade* measure more like 211m. Procopius is not, however, consistent in his measurement of a *stade* and he can make a *stade* up to 250m (which may, admittedly, be a scribal error). Nevertheless, exact measurements are impossible, especially because the precise locations of some places mentioned in Procopius' text are not known and other modern equivalents give various breakdowns. (Rais67/Wikimedia/Public Domain)

On the same day, Gelimer placed his nephew Gibamundus in command of 2,000 Vandal cavalry and instructed him to go ahead of the main Vandal army on the left (3.18.1). In this way, Gelimer's net was spread. Gelimer was in the rear with his main force; Bury estimates (1889: 134) that he left the road pursuing Belisarius at modern-day Grombalia, Tunisia, seeking to keep Belisarius between himself and the coast. Ammatas was coming from Carthage, and Gibamundus from the left. They would all combine to encircle Belisarius and trap him against the coast. At this point (3.18.2), Procopius inserts himself into the narrative once more, to wonder at Belisarius' dispositions of troops under John and the Huns. He conjectures that if they had not been arranged in such a way, 'we should never have been able to escape the Vandals' (3.18.3). Despite telling us of Belisarius' dispositions for the march, it seems that Procopius did not understand their meaning or indeed the foresight and preparedness they revealed in Belisarius' knowing just what Gelimer would attempt.

Even with this forward planning by Belisarius, Procopius notes (3.18.3–4) that the Vandals could still have won, but then ruins any sense of drama by telling us (3.18.4) that Ammatas got his timing wrong by arriving at Ad Decimum at about midday (somewhat ahead of the time agreed) while both the Vandal army and the Byzantines were still some way off; Procopius claims (3.18.4) he mistimed his arrival by a quarter of a day. Ammatas had also left a large number of men at Carthage in order that he could get to Ad Decimum as quickly as possible and the troops he brought were not the best troops at his disposal. Bury speculates (1889: 133) – probably correctly – that Ammatas was surveying the ground rather than arriving early with insufficient and inappropriate troops.

As a result of Ammatas' presence, John, riding ahead of Belisarius' column as instructed, came up against a smaller and weaker force of Vandals under Ammatas than could have been expected. John's cavalry therefore attacked this small force, although the Byzantine commander may still have been outnumbered. Ammatas, fighting in the front rank, showed himself to be

After marching to Leptis (modern-day Monastir, Tunisia), Belisarius' march reached Hadrumentum, the ruins of which can be seen here. It is now a suburb of the city of Sousse (formerly the village of Hammeim), Tunisia. It had been renamed Honoropolis after the Western Roman Emperor Honorius I (r. 393–423) in the early 5th century, then Hunericopolis by the Vandal King Huneric (r. 477–84) – although it suffered damage in 434 when the Vandals conquered it – and lastly Justinianopolis by Justinian I, but Procopius refers to it by the name which pre-dates all of these. (Habib M'henni/ Wikimedia/CC BY-SA 3.0)

brave and killed 12 of John's best men before he fell (3.18.6). The remainder of his men were then utterly routed; 'fleeing at top speed' (3.18.7), they were joined by all those men who were still heading to Ad Decimum from Carthage. These men, who had been advancing not in battle order, nor in any organized way, but in small groups, joined the rout and were pursued by John's men, who killed all they came upon in their pursuit, reaching the gates of Carthage itself (3.18.10). Procopius summarizes that so great was the 'slaughter of Vandals in the course of seventy *stadia* [back to Carthage] that those who beheld it would have supposed that it was the work of an enemy twenty thousand strong' (3.18.11). John only had 300 *bucellarii* at his disposal (less the 12 killed by Ammatas).

While Ammatas was being routed at Ad Decimum, Gibamundus reached the Pedion Halon 'salt plain', some 40 *stadia* (7.4–8.4km) west of Ad Decimum. There, at a place without trees or water, his force was met by the Huns (3.18.12). Bury contends (1889: 133) that the Huns were headed to Sidi Fathalla (close to modern-day Jebel Jeloud, Tunis) when they came across Gibamundus' force. Despite their numerical disadvantage (600 versus 2,000), the Hunnic force destroyed the Vandals under Gibamundus. The Vandals broke and fled 'never thinking of resistance', and all were 'disgracefully destroyed' (3.18.19). Given that the Huns were all horse-archers and capable of mêlée, it is likely that the Vandals could not withstand an archery barrage followed up with a hand-to-hand charge. Nor could they reply with archery of their own.

Meanwhile, the troops in Belisarius' column knew nothing of either John's or the Huns' success. Seeing a suitable place for a camp some 35 *stadia* (6.5–7.4km) from Ad Decimum – perhaps at Hammam el-Enf (modern-day Hammam Lif, Tunisia) – Belisarius had the site surrounded with a stockade within which he placed his infantry (3.19.1). He gathered the army and spoke to them (3.19.2–10), stating that the decisive moment was at hand. The fleet was gone and they were alone in a hostile environment and could trust only in their own strength. He emphasized that justice was on their side (something he had reiterated earlier) and spoke of 'the hatred of the Vandals toward their own tyrant' (3.19.5). He also stated (3.19.7) – perhaps Procopius used hindsight here – that the Vandals had been idle, fighting only 'naked' Berbers, and would therefore be inefficient whereas his men were all veterans of Persian and Scythian campaigns.

Having made this speech, Belisarius left the infantry (and his wife) in camp and rode out with all his remaining cavalry (3.19.11). Procopius' judgement is that Belisarius did not want to risk a battle with his entire army but only sought a skirmish to 'make trial of the enemy's strength' (3.19.12). Once this had been achieved, he could fight a battle with his whole army, knowing what forces he was up against. He sent forward the commanders of his *foederati* – Solomon, Cyprian, Valerian, Martinus, Althias, John the Armenian and Marcellus; Dorotheus had died on Sicily and Cyril had been sent to Sardinia (3.11.1, 3.24.19). Each of the seven commanders probably had a contingent of 400 men, so 2,800 men in total. Belisarius followed on behind the *foederati* with his spear-armed cavalry and his remaining bodyguard horsemen, some 1,200 men (3.19.13). When the *foederati* reached Ad Decimum, they saw the evidence of the slaughter of Gibamundus' force – the 12 men from John's force and then the bodies of Ammatas and his Vandals. Locals told them the story of the fight and they were unsure of what to do next (3.19.14–15). A dust cloud appeared from the south, however, which proved to denote a large force of Vandal horsemen. The *foederati* sent word to Belisarius that he should come as soon as possible (3.19.16).

The *foederati* commanders were divided in their opinions – some contended that they should ride out and close with the Vandals, while others argued that they did not have sufficient numbers to undertake such an engagement

A mounted hunter with a round shield and a spear from a 4th–5th-century mosaic from the villa of Las Tiendas, Emerita Augusta (modern-day Mérida, Spain), and now held in the National Museum of Roman Art, Mérida, Spain. (Luis Rogelio HM - Merida - 107/Wikimedia/CC BY-SA 2.0)

(3.19.17). The Vandals drew nearer and were, in fact, commanded by Gelimer himself. He had been pursuing Belisarius along a route running between the coastal route taken by Belisarius' column and that taken by the Huns further inland. Bury suggests (1889: 134) – probably accurately – that Gelimer was proceeding overland from modern-day Grombalia, Tunisia, keeping west of the hills at Jebel Bu-Kornin (now the Boukornine National Park). The terrain was hilly and so Gelimer did not know of the disaster that had befallen Gibamundus on his left; nor did he realize that Belisarius had erected a fortified camp or that Belisarius was still advancing towards Ad Decimum on his right (3.19.18–19). Gelimer's cavalry engaged with those of the *foederati* at Ad Decimum, fighting for possession of the hills there (3.19.20–21). Tissot and Bury's suggested site near Jebel Jeloud had just such hills; Bury suggests (1889: 134) Megrin as a location for this action. The Vandals got the better of this engagement and the *foederati* withdrew seven *stadia* (1.3–1.5km) back towards Belisarius' column (3.19.22–23). There they were met by Uliaris, the personal guard of Belisarius, with 800 *bucellarii* (3.19.23). Procopius reports (3.19.24) that the *foederati* expected to renew the attack with these reinforcements but, contrary to that expectation, the whole force instead made its way back to Belisarius.

Procopius states (3.19.25) that Gelimer had victory in his hands but surrendered it; this judgement seems harsh, as both Ammatas and Gibamundus were utterly defeated – the latter despite a clear numerical superiority – and the encircling net Gelimer had planned was already torn apart. Still, Procopius supposes that, if Gelimer had pursued the retreating horsemen, 'I do not think that even Belisarius would have withstood him, but our cause would have been utterly and completely lost' (3.19.26). The implication here is that Gelimer's forces still outnumbered those of Belisarius. Procopius also judges (3.19.27) that if Gelimer had ridden on to Carthage, he

A 6th-century mosaic of a rider using a spear one-handed from the Great Palace, Constantinople. The techniques honed in hunting (shown much more often in mosaics than military subjects) will have been largely the same as those used in war. Where we see military themes on gravestones and other art, they are identical. (PRISMA ARCHIVO/Alamy Stock Photo)

The Zaghouan aqueduct, shown here, provided Carthage with water. After the battle of Ad Decimum and the Byzantine capture of the city, the Vandals ravaged the area around Carthage in the hope that it would be betrayed to them. They also destroyed sections of the aqueduct. This section of the aqueduct, which brought water to the city from 132km away, shows obvious signs of repair. (Pawel Kowalczyk/ Alamy Stock Photo)

could have destroyed John's small force of *bucellarii*, the members of which had already dispersed and were stripping the dead. Instead, Gelimer walked his force down from the hill and, seeing his brother's corpse, intended to give him a proper burial. Procopius' judgement is accurate: 'he blunted the edge of his opportunity – an opportunity he was not able to grasp again' (3.19.29). Bury's judgement that his brother's death 'completely unmanned' Gelimer (1889: 135) also sounds plausible. It is possible, however, that Gelimer thought he had won the engagement when the *foederati* withdrew and that he had defeated Belisarius' forces.

Meeting the fleeing cavalry as he advanced from the camp – perhaps at a spot close to modern-day Ez Zahra, Tunisia – Belisarius brought them to a stop and rebuked them. He then learned of Ammatas' death and the pursuit of John's *bucellarii* and immediately made to advance with all haste against the Vandals (3.19.30). The Vandals, however, had already broken ranks to see to the dead and they fled in response to the Byzantines' charge; many were killed and only nightfall (around 1830hrs) brought an end to the killing (3.19.31). The rout of the Vandals was complete: they did not flee to Carthage or Byzacena but to the Plain of Boulla (probably around the area of Bulla Regia, near modern-day Jendouba, Tunisia), and the road leading into Numidia (3.19.32). At around the time this final rout took place, both John with his *bucellarii* and the Huns returned to Ad Decimum where the combined cavalry force of the Byzantines spent the night. The Vandal kingdom had been broken in the space of only six hours.

The following day, the infantry advanced to Ad Decimum and then the united force moved on to Carthage, which was reached late in the evening of the day following the battle. The city opened its gates to Belisarius, any remaining Vandals having taken refuge in the city's churches (3.20.1). Belisarius suspected some trick and did not allow his men to enter the city; this also prevented them from plundering it. The fleet had also reached the Mandracium harbour and had been allowed to enter, the chain in the harbour having been removed by the suppliant city, although the Byzantine sailors also suspected a trick and moved on instead to the harbour of Stagnum, 40 *stadia* from the city (3.20.15). Despite Belisarius' orders, however, the admiral Calonymus took some men and plundered the Mandracium harbour.

Tricamarum

15 December AD 533

BACKGROUND TO BATTLE

The day after the battle of Ad Decimum, both the Byzantine army and navy reached Carthage; Belisarius ordered the troops to disembark from the ships and he paraded the entire army in battle formation (Procopius, 3.20.17). Belisarius warned them of potential enemy ambushes and reminded them to not behave violently towards the Carthaginians. They then marched into Carthage and encountered not a single enemy. Belisarius marched straight to Gelimer's palace, where a crowd of merchants complained of the harbour looting the previous night. Belisarius tasked the admiral Calonymus with finding the perpetrators, not knowing it was Calonymus himself who was the guilty party. (Procopius foreshadows that Calonymus got away with his crimes, but was later punished in Constantinople, where he became diseased with apoplexy and bit off his own tongue and died – 3.20.24–25.)

Belisarius dined in Gelimer's palace, served by the slaves of the Vandal usurper. Procopius indulges in hyperbole by stating that it fell to Belisarius 'to win such fame as no one of the men of his time ever won nor indeed any of the men of olden times' (3.21.8). Procopius also praises the discipline of Belisarius' troops: 'all the soldiers under command of this general showed themselves so orderly that there was not a single act of insolence nor a threat, and indeed nothing happened to hinder the business of the city' (3.21.9–10). As the intention was to bring Carthage back into the empire, this restraint was necessary but also admirably accomplished by Belisarius, and the anecdotes of his disciplining the troops (Calonymus notwithstanding) show how it was his intention from the start that the campaign be conducted in this way. Belisarius issued proclamations that the Vandals who had fled to the Arian churches would be unharmed and began to think about repairing the fortifications of the city.

The Mosaic of Dominus Julius from Carthage is a late 4th- or early 5th-century scene that shows how much of the city would have looked when taken by the Vandals and then repaired by Belisarius. As soon as he entered the city, Belisarius began to repair the walls. They had been neglected and were in disrepair – the reason Gelimer had not made a stand in the city (3.21.12). Belisarius employed local workmen to dig a trench around the wall of Carthage and built a palisade so that he could repair the walls uninterrupted (3.23.19–20). When Gelimer was finally taken captive in 534 he marvelled at this work and saw that his own neglect to undertake such work himself had been his undoing (3.23.21). The details of dress and daily life in Carthage remained largely unchanged under Vandal occupation. (DEA/G. DAGLI ORTI/Getty Images)

During this period, Gelimer had retreated into the Libyan countryside. He distributed money to the local population and encouraged them to kill any Romans who ventured out (3.23.1). This the locals did, being paid a fixed sum for each man killed (they presented the decapitated heads of their victims as proof). Procopius tells us that they killed many, 'not soldiers, however, but slaves and servants, who because of a desire for money went up into the villages stealthily and were caught' (3.23.3); Belisarius too sent men to spy on the Vandals (3.23.5–18).

Meanwhile, Gelimer's other brother, Tzazon, had invaded Sardinia, which had revolted from Vandal control under the leadership of Godas (Procopius, 3.11.23). Tzazon, with 120 ships and 5,000 troops took the harbour of Caranalis (modern-day Cagliari, Sardinia) and killed Godas (3.24.1). Learning of Belisarius' expedition (but not its rapid and overwhelming success), Tzazon wrote to Gelimer; his couriers were apprehended as they entered Carthage's harbour, however, completely unaware that the city had fallen to Belisarius (3.24.2–5). Belisarius thus learned that Sardinia had fallen to the Vandals, but he did nothing to punish the couriers.

In addition to the expedition to Sardinia, Gelimer had also sent envoys to Spain to persuade the ruler of the Visigoths there to enter into an alliance. This was Theudis (r. 531–48), a figure Procopius deals with more fully in his material on the later Gothic Wars (5.12.50–54). The Vandal envoys had, however, travelled slowly and such was the rapidity of Belisarius' success that Theudis had already learned (from a merchant ship which arrived the day of the envoys' arrival) of the fall of Carthage. Theudis, therefore, entertained Gelimer's envoys but refused to enter into an alliance. Learning of the fate of Carthage, the envoys returned and surrendered to Belisarius (3.24.7–18). Cyril, who had been sent by Justinian I to Sardinia, learned of Tzazon's conquest and came to Carthage (3.24.19), adding his 400 men to Belisarius' forces. Another of Belisarius' *foederati* commanders, Solomon, was sent to Constantinople to announce the victory to Justinian I. An amazing coincidence at this point tells us just how rapid travel could be in the Mediterranean. Before the campaign (3.10.14), John the Cappadocian complained that it would take a whole year to learn of anything that happened in North Africa. The battle of Ad Decimum was fought on 15 September and Solomon was sent to Constantinople soon after. By 21 November that year, a little more than two months after the battle, Justinian I could dedicate the first edition of his *Institutes* (Proemium) to the victory achieved in North Africa. In that Proemium, Justinian I took the titles of *Vandalicus* and *Africanus*.

After Gelimer reached the Plain of Boulla – four days' travel for an unencumbered traveller (Procopius 3.25.1) – close to the border with Numidia, he gathered his remaining forces and as many Berber troops (Procopius uses the term 'Moor' – *Maurousioi* in Greek) as he could. The Berbers were, however, reluctant to join him: their leaders had sent envoys to Belisarius promising to serve with him (3.25.2–3) and they sent Belisarius their children as hostages to show their sincerity. In the event, the Berbers did not fight alongside Belisarius as promised, but neither did they fight with the Vandals (3.24.9), instead waiting to see the outcome of the contest.

Gelimer also wrote to Tzazon in Sardinia, not knowing of his brother's success or his letter (3.25.10), claiming that 'it was not to recover the island for us that you sailed from here, but in order that Justinian might be master of Libya' (3.25.13). Gelimer complained that 'Belisarius, then, has come against us with a small army, but valour straightway departed and fled from the Vandals, taking good fortune with her' (3.25.14). He informed Tzazon of their brother Ammatas' death and of Gibamundus', adding that 'the Vandals lost their courage, and the horses and shipyards and all Libya and, not least of all, Carthage itself' (3.25.15). Gelimer urged Tzazon to return as soon as possible from Sardinia, and to bring his whole force with him; with them, Gelimer intended to recover their fortunes or, at least, to be together to share what fate had in store.

Tzazon received the letter and made immediate preparations to return (3.25.19). He sailed with his whole fleet, reaching the boundary between Numidia and Mauretania on the third day (3.25.21), then marching to the Plain of Boulla. There is some real humanity in Procopius' story of the brothers Gelimer and Tzazon's meeting – they had lost a brother and a nephew (3.25.24–26) and it is with this incident that Procopius' first book of the Vandalic War ends. The second book begins with Gelimer leading all of his now-combined remaining forces against Carthage (4.1.1). This advance would culminate in the battle of Tricamarum.

ABOVE LEFT
The ruins of Bulla Regia (modern-day Jendouba, Tunisia). The Plain of Boulla was where Gelimer retreated to after the battle of Ad Decimum, on the road to Numidia, before advancing on Carthage again and then withdrawing the way he came, only to be defeated a second time at the battle of Tricamarum, just 30km from Carthage. (Pascal Radigue/ Wikimedia/CC BY-SA 3.0)

ABOVE RIGHT
Despite having a reputation only for destruction, the surviving remains of the Vandal Empire (such as Carthage, depicted here) reveal that the Vandals preserved much of what they found. The survival (and even creation) of mosaics and Arian churches tells a different story than the word 'vandal' evokes. What is more, certain features such as the aqueduct system, which was essential to life in Carthage, were maintained during the century of Vandal control. (Juha Puikkonen/Alamy Stock Photo)

MAP KEY

1   Gelimer and Tzazon, newly strengthened by Tzazon's 5,000 Sardinian veterans, lead their army out around midday, arraying themselves on the northern bank of the stream. Tzazon with his 5,000 Sardinian veterans is in the centre (**A**). To his right (**B**) and left (**C**), the remainder of the Vandals (perhaps 25,000 men divided equally left and right) are drawn up. Gelimer roams the lines encouraging his men. The Vandals are armed only with their swords.

2   Belisarius deploys his men with the *foederati* cavalry on the left wing (**D**). These consisted of units of roughly 400 men each under Martinus, Valerian, John the Armenian, Cyprian, Althias, Marcellus and other commanders (approximately 2,000 men in total). The 600 Huns (**E**), commanded by Sinnion and Balas (although they have not been named since 3.11.11), are leftmost, and separated from the other cavalry. The right wing (**F**) consists of the remaining cavalry (in units of 500 men) commanded by Pappas, Barbatus and others (1,500 men in total). In the centre, the infantry (**G**) are stationed advancing at a walk, and ahead of them John commands a force of *bucellarii* and regular cavalry with Belisarius' standard, perhaps 1,100 men (**H**). Next to John in the centre and in front of the slowly advancing infantry, Belisarius (**I**) is positioned with 500 *bucellarii*.

3   John leads forward a selected group of *bucellarii* and regular cavalry, who charge Tzazon in the Vandal centre. This charge is repulsed (perhaps in feigned retreat) and the cavalry retire back to the Byzantine camp. Tzazon prevents his troops from pursuing.

4   John leads a second selected group of *bucellarii* and regular cavalry who repeat the same tactic and who, again, withdraw back to the Byzantine camp. Again, Tzazon prevents his men from pursuing.

5   John leads a third charge with all the remaining *bucellarii* and regular cavalry and taking the standard of Belisarius forward against Tzazon in the Vandal centre. A fierce fight erupts in the centre.

6   Tzazon, in the Vandal centre, falls while fighting. The entire Byzantine army advances across the stream.

7   The Vandals do not put up much of a fight but, disheartened at the defeat of Tzazon, give way soon after the Byzantine forces reach them. The Huns join the pursuit of the defeated Vandals.

Battlefield environment

Procopius tells us (4.2.4) that Tricamarum was 150 *stadia* (27.8–31.6km) from Carthage. This gives us a radius of some 30km from Carthage but presumably, the Vandals retreated the way they came, so towards modern-day Oued Ellil, Sanhaja or Borj Chekir, on the outskirts of modern-day Tunis. The battlefield may have been built over during the development of Tunis and the stream on which Procopius says the battle was fought may not provide us much additional detail. He adds that, despite having a constant flow, 'its volume is so small that it is not even given a special name by the inhabitants of the place, but it is designated simply as a brook' (4.3.2). This might describe the Medjerda River, however, which is the only constantly flowing river in the region today and which does indeed pass close to Oued Ellil, Sanhaja and Borj Chekir to the west. This observation is, however, complicated by the fact that later (4.15.13), Procopius names the Bagradas River (the Medjerda); it is possible he did not connect the two, or that it was indeed simply referred to as 'the stream' by locals. Unlike the detailed analysis by Tissot and Bury for Ad Decimum, no similar detail is forthcoming for Tricamarum – only that it is on the Medjerda but unidentified. There are some clues as to where we might look

for the battlefield, assuming the terrain has remained relatively unchanged. Given that John reportedly charged across the river relatively unimpeded, we should look for a place where the banks are not steep and where they might suit such a charge (on three occasions). Similarly, the Byzantine side should also be sought where tempting the Vandals to pursue was also a viable option. A relatively flat plain where the river meanders through the landscape rather than cutting through it would seem to suit the action of the battle best.

After the battle, the defeated Vandals retreated, not back towards Bulla Regia, but towards Hippo Regius (modern-day Annaba, Algeria). The route towards Hippo Regius and that back to the Plain of Boulla was probably the same one – and the new destination was probably predicated on escape by sea. John pursued the defeated Vandals for five days (perhaps 200km) and then Belisarius continued the pursuit, learning that Gelimer had taken refuge on Mount Pappas while many others had claimed sanctuary in Hippo Regius. It makes sense therefore that Mount Pappas was close to Hippo Regius; Mount Edough, near Annaba, is a good candidate. The Berber city of Medeos remains unidentified.

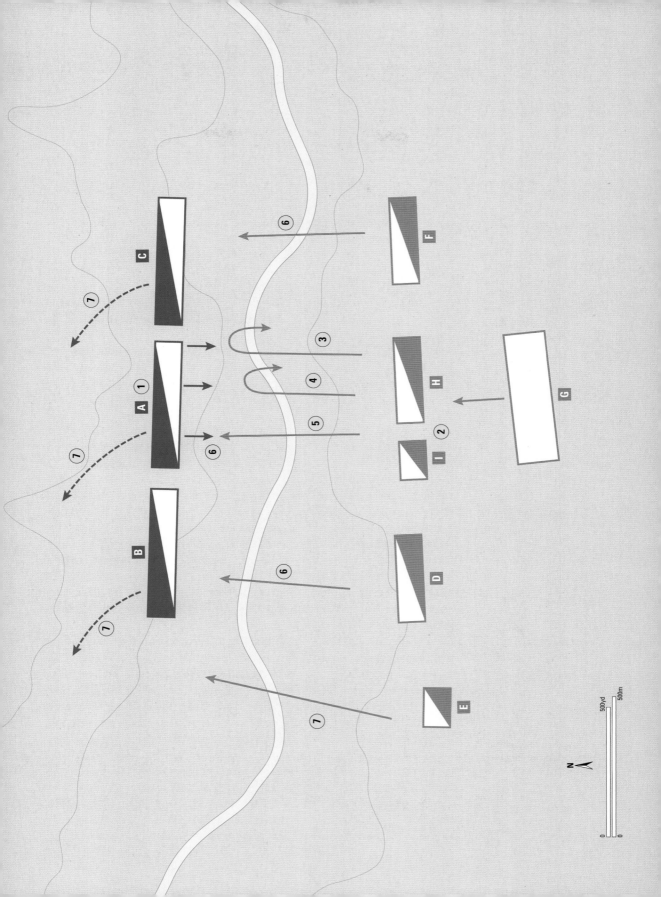

INTO COMBAT

Advancing towards Carthage from the Plain of Boulla, the Vandals tore down part of the aqueduct which provided the city with essential water. They patrolled the roads around Carthage, plundering the vicinity, as if the city was under siege, but no force came out. Procopius tells us (4.1.4) that the Vandals hoped someone in the city would betray it to them, but this did not happen. Seeing the repairs to the walls of Carthage, and finding no betrayal of the city to them, they withdrew towards Tricamarum, 150 *stadia* (27.8–31.6km).

Much of the conflict between the Vandals and the local North Africans is presented in terms of a conflict between Arian and Nicene Christianity. The Vandals had been converted to Arianism soon after crossing into the Roman Empire in the 4th century and they retained this faith. Since the death of the Eastern Roman Emperor Valens (r. 364–78) in 378, however, Nicene – Orthodox – Christianity had been ascendant in both halves of the Roman Empire. Gelimer also made an appeal to the leadership of the Huns, promising to pay them handsomely if they joined in alliance with the Vandals. According to Procopius (4.1.5–6), the Huns were sympathetic to these appeals and promised that 'when they should come to real fighting they would turn against the Roman army' (4.1.6). Belisarius, however, was aware of the Hunnic perfidy (and made his own efforts to retain their loyalty). He was also still completing the repairs to Carthage's walls behind its palisade and trench. For these reasons he sent no force out to meet the Vandals, but made preparations inside the city. He had also impaled a criminal on a charge of treason in a prominent position (just as he had done with the two Hun murderers at Abydos) and this kept the population fearful and reluctant to assist the Vandals (4.1.8). Belisarius learned that the Huns feared that they would not be permitted to return to their homes if the Vandals were defeated, but would be compelled to stay in Libya. Belisarius promised that he would send them home without delay once the Vandals were defeated (4.1.10–11).

Having secured the loyalty of the Huns and completed the repairs to Carthage's walls, Belisarius gathered his whole army and spoke to them (4.1.13–25), encouraging them as the conquerors of Carthage to end the Vandal threat once and for all. Having spoken to them, he sent all his cavalry, leaving only 500 cavalrymen and the bodyguard (perhaps his 1,100 *bucellarii*) with the standard (4.2.1). Procopius tells us the standard was called the *bandum* (*bandon* in Greek) – this was the *vexillum praetorium* carried by guard cavalry (*pannum* in Latin). The cavalry were entrusted to John and instructed to skirmish only if the opportunity arose. The following day, Belisarius left the city with his entire infantry force and the remaining cavalry (4.2.2). The Huns were in two minds because they had received assurances from both Belisarius and the Vandals and so decided to see how the conflict played out before deciding whether they would remain loyal to the Byzantines or go over to the Vandals (4.2.3).

Belisarius' advance brought him to the Vandal camp at Tricamarum where the armies camped some distance from each other. In the night, Procopius reports an omen in which 'the tips of their spears were lighted with a bright fire and the points of them seemed to be burning most vigorously' (4.2.6). This was probably the electrostatic phenomenon of St Elmo's Fire, which had

been observed before (Caesar, *Civil Wars* (*African War*) 4.47), although the reporting of such an omen might be intended to connect Belisarius with the previous battles at which it had happened (Caesar's forces facing the armies of King Juba in 46 BC). This linking of an omen before a Belisarius battle and Julius Caesar's final victory in North Africa in the civil wars was as much literary as it was actual – Procopius even tells us the phenomenon was 'not seen by many' (4.2.6). This connection with Caesar may also be a reason for a strength of 80,000 men being attributed to the Vandals by Procopius: Vercingetorix, the chieftain of the Averni who revolted against Caesar in 52 BC, also had 80,000 men at Alesia (Caesar, *Gallic Wars* 7.71) and this may have been a deliberate parallel. Although the comparison is not explicit, there are several aspects of Belisarius' generalship (as presented by Procopius) that echo those of Caesar – notably a series of rapid marches and successfully attacking superior forces with his own, trusted veterans.

Gelimer placed the women and children within the stockade of his camp and spoke to his army (4.2.9–22). He exhorted them to regain the Vandal realm or else perish. Tzazon then spoke separately to his Sardinian veterans (4.2.24–32), encouraging the re-conquerors of Sardinia to add more valorous deeds to those they had already achieved. Unlike Gelimer's forces, Tzazon's men had not recently met with defeat and so had the chance to be seen as the 'saviours of the nation of the Vandals' (4.2.30).

Gelimer and Tzazon then led their army out at around lunchtime (4.3.1), a move reportedly unexpected by the Romans, either because they had seen no action earlier in the day or because Procopius wishes to play up the drama.

The Vandals favoured simple forms of the *spangenhelm* such as this 5th–6th-century bronze example from Eastern Europe, with riveted silver plates. The interior view shows the helmet's ridges. Helmets would have had internal padding although this kind of material seldom survives. (INTERFOTO/Alamy Stock Photo)

According to Procopius (4.3.2–3), the Vandals arrayed themselves for battle along the bank of a stream, but one so small that it was not given a special name by the locals. The Romans came to the opposite bank and arrayed themselves. Procopius goes into some detail regarding the Roman deployment. The left wing was made up of *foederati* (4.3.4); Procopius names Martinus, Valerian, John the Armenian, Cyprian, Althias and Marcellus among the *foederati* commanders. The right wing consisted of cavalry commanded by 'Pappas, Barbatus, and Aïgan, and the others who commanded the forces of cavalry' (4.3.4). In the centre, John commanded 'the guards [*doryphoroi*] and spearmen [*upaspistai*] of Belisarius and carrying the general's standard' (4.3.5). Belisarius was also in the centre commanding 500 *bucellarii*. The infantry were deployed some way behind the cavalry in the centre, 'advancing at a walk' (4.3.6). The Huns were standing separate from the other forces as was normal: 'arrayed in another place' is Procopius' phrase (4.3.7), although we can compare their entirely separate action at the battle of Ad Decimum. This was probably on the extreme left with the other *foederati* cavalry.

The Vandals drew up their line with Tzazon in the centre, presumably with his 5,000 men; on each of the wings were the *chiliarchoi*, each one leading a division (*lochos*) (4.3.8). These were probably equally split left and right of Tzazon. Gelimer 'was going about everywhere exhorting them and urging them on to daring' (4.3.9), presumably, like Belisarius, accompanied by an elite unit of cavalry. Procopius tells us that 'the command had been previously given to all the Vandals to use neither spear nor any other weapon in this engagement except their swords' (4.3.9). Gibbon (1788: 634) thought that they discarded their lances and missile weapons; he seems to have been unable to accept that they fought without missile weapons.

A considerable time passed with no movement (4.3.10), but, at length, John chose a force (already suggested by Belisarius) for the river crossing, and these men made an attack on the Vandal centre. Procopius only tells us that there were 'a few' (4.3.10). Tzazon stopped their advance, forced them to retire and chased them. Although the Byzantines retired to their camp, Tzazon

A two-part iron riveted helmet dating from the 6th or 7th centuries; originally, it probably also had cheek pieces attached. Many simple, undecorated helmet designs such as this one would have been worn by the majority of Vandal troops. (INTERFOTO/Alamy Stock Photo)

stopped his pursuit at the stream (4.3.11). The Byzantine force may have been instructed to withdraw to their camp, perhaps as an example of the tactic of feigned retreat (which Roman armies had encountered fighting the Huns in the 5th century). This force may have been attempting to lure Tzazon and the Vandal centre to pursue too far and cross the stream.

John now selected a second force of *bucellarii* and attacked Tzazon again (4.3.12), but once more this was repulsed, and they again withdrew to the Byzantine camp. With these feints unsuccessful, a third attack was mounted. This time John advanced with 'almost all the guards and spearmen of Belisarius'; he took 'the general's standard and made his attack with much shouting and a great noise' (4.3.13). This was still an attack at poor odds (at least on paper). John had perhaps 1,000 cavalry and was leading them against 5,000. It is therefore probable that John had heavy cavalry – the *bucellarii*, *cataphractarii* and *clibanarii*. The Vandals, however, withstood the attack and, using only their swords as instructed 'the battle became fierce, and many of the noblest of the Vandals fell, and among them Tzazon himself' (4.3.14). This may have been the moment the Byzantine commanders had been waiting for, as now we are told the 'whole Roman army was set in motion' (4.3.15). They crossed the stream and advanced on the Vandal centre, which, without Tzazon, soon gave way. The remainder of the Vandal army soon followed, 'for each of the Roman divisions turned to flight those before them with no trouble' (4.3.15).

On seeing this rout, only then did the Huns join the Byzantine forces in the pursuit of the defeated Vandals. Procopius' accounts of both sides' attempted wooing of the Huns, and the Huns' prevarication, may have been intended to explain why they had played so little part in the battle to that

The final charge at Tricamarum

John, Belisarius' trusted cavalry commander, leads a third charge at the Vandal centre against the 5,000 Sardinian veterans of Tzazon, the Vandal king Gelimer's brother. Tzazon's men have come from the successful re-conquest of Sardinia and have not tasted defeat, unlike Gelimer's forces at the battle of Ad Decimum. Tzazon's forces have already withstood two charges on the banks of the Bagradas River. They have also not been duped by the feigned retreat of those two earlier charges, intended to make them cross the river and pursue the retiring Byzantine cavalry and so disrupt the Vandal line. John leads the remaining *bucellarii* and other heavy cavalry along with the standard of Belisarius, the *strategon de autokratora* ('with supreme authority over all' – Procopius, 3.11.18). Now the battle will be decided in a fierce contest of combat on the riverbank. The remainder of the Vandal army await the outcome of this conflict while the rest of Belisarius' forces, 3,500 cavalry and 10,000 infantry, follow John's advance.

point and only joined in late. (At the battle of Ad Decimum they had played an important part early in the battle on the left flank against Gibamundus.) It is possible that no such offer and counter-offer took place, but something made Procopius interpret their inaction here until late in the battle as being evidence of suspect loyalty. The Huns' numbers may have been depleted after the battle of Ad Decimum, where they performed extraordinary service despite being significantly outnumbered, and so they may not have been required in the Tricamarum battle plan.

The Vandals returned to their camp and, although Procopius was dismissive of its construction and effectiveness as a fort (4.2.8), the Roman pursuit was halted and no assault on the camp was made (4.3.17). Procopius estimates that the Romans lost only 50 men whereas the Vandals lost 800 (4.3.18).

Bury is right to call the battle of Tricamarum 'a battle of cavalry' (1889: 136). Procopius tells us that the infantry were 'advancing at a walk' (4.3.6) and only arrived when the battle was already decided. When the Byzantine infantry came up in the late afternoon, they moved against the Vandal camp (4.3.19). Procopius relates (4.3.1) that the Vandals deployed at midday and that a considerable period of inaction ensued, so this move need not have been significantly later than the battle. According to Procopius (4.3.20–21), seeing this, Gelimer immediately mounted a horse and fled towards Numidia, followed by only a few kinsmen and some domestics. The remainder of the Vandals were initially unaware of Gelimer's flight, but Procopius claims (4.3.22–23) that on realizing that the Vandal king had departed, his troops also fled in complete disorder, leaving their treasures and their wives and children in the camp. This is an exaggeration since in the following sentence, Procopius states that Vandal women and children encountered on the pursuit were made into slaves (4.3.24). The Byzantine forces, therefore, came upon a camp without a man in it but found much wealth, plundered from the province since before Belisarius' arrival. The Byzantines pursued the fleeing Vandals until nightfall. Procopius makes the point that this victory was achieved only three months after Belisarius took Carthage 'at about the middle of the last month, which the Romans call "December"' (4.3.28).

In the face of so much plunder present in the Vandal camp, Byzantine discipline disintegrated. Belisarius realized that if the Vandals rallied and returned, they could cause great harm to his army (4.4.1). Seeing so much wealth, the Byzantine troops began to seize plunder and slaves and, splitting into twos and threes, they took their new-found wealth back to Carthage (4.4.3–4). In victory, Belisarius was unable to restore the discipline he had built when the result was still in doubt. At dawn the following day, he took position on a hill and reproached the men for their ill-discipline (4.4.7). Some, especially his own household troops, sent the booty back to Carthage with others and drew up in formation near Belisarius.

John was given 200 cavalry to continue the pursuit of Gelimer (4.4.9) and ordered to take him alive or dead. Belisarius also sent word back to Carthage that all the Vandals still in sanctuary in the churches should be gathered together and their weapons confiscated, but given pledges that no harm would come to them (4.4.10–12). This was done to avoid an uprising of the Vandals still in Carthage and those around it who had also sought sanctuary since the defeat. Once these arrangements were made and confirmed, and men sent to act as guards, Belisarius too set off in pursuit of Gelimer himself (4.4.13).

John, after five days and nights of pursuit, had already drawn close to Gelimer and was set to attack him the following day (4.4.14). In the night, however, a hunting accident resulted in John being injured in the neck (4.4.15–23). The men broke off the pursuit to tend to John's wound (and reported back to Belisarius). The perpetrator of the accident, Uliaris, the same bodyguard of Belisarius who had led 800 *bucellarii* at the battle of Ad Decimum, sought sanctuary in a church. Belisarius, learning of John's death, rushed to be present for his burial and Procopius laments the loss of a great officer (4.4.19–20). John had been instrumental at the battles of Ad Decimum and Tricamarum and his loss was immense. Belisarius did not, however, punish Uliaris (4.4.25).

The loss of John did mean that Gelimer escaped and when Belisarius reached the town of Hippo Regius (modern-day Annaba, Algeria), ten days' journey from Carthage, he learned (4.4.26–27) that Gelimer had taken refuge on Mount Pappas (or Mount Papua – the location is unidentified although it could be Mount Edough, near Annaba, a precipitous mountain on the border of Numidia where it would be impossible to pursue). Bury posits that Gelimer fled further away, into the 'wilds of Numidia' (1889: 136). Gelimer was being sheltered in the Berber city of Medeos (a city which defies identification) on the side of the mountain. More Vandals had taken refuge as suppliants in the churches of Hippo Regius whom Belisarius would send back to Carthage (4.4.32).

As it was already late December, Belisarius could not continue the pursuit and, what is more, he thought that to be away from Carthage too much longer was inadvisable (4.4.28). He therefore tasked Pharas and selected soldiers – among whom were some of his own lineage from the Herulians – to maintain a siege of the mountain (4.4.29). Procopius makes a point of telling us that Pharas and the men who followed him were the exceptions to the Herulians in general, who were less than reliable: 'for an Herulian not to give himself over to treachery and drunkenness, but to strive after uprightness, is no easy matter and merits abundant praise' (4.4.30). There were 1,000

Belisarius

Belisarius was born in 'Germania, which lies between Thrace and Illyricum' (Procopius 3.11.21) probably around 500 and rose to be a bodyguard cavalryman (*doryphoros*) of the Eastern Roman Emperor Justin I (r. 518–27). Sent to the East, he experienced defeat in 528 but in 529 was appointed *magister militum per Orientem* (master of soldiers of the East) and won the battle of Dara in 530, but lost the battle of Callinicum in 531. The 'Endless Peace' with Persia was signed in September 532 and Belisarius was sent to North Africa in June 533 where he triumphed against all the odds in a lightning-fast campaign.

In 535, Belisarius occupied Sicily and invaded Italy. In 536, after another rapid victory in North Africa, he marched on Naples and entered Rome on 9 December. There, he was besieged and defeated in 537, but held out and in 538 he took Arminium (modern-day Rimini, Italy) and Mediolanum (modern-day Milan, Italy). In 540 he was offered the kingship of Italy – which he refused,

although the offer led to uncertainty about his loyalty – and took Ravenna, capturing the Ostrogoth king, Witigis.

Recalled to fight in the East, Belisarius fought at Nisibis (modern-day Nusaybin, Turkey) and Sisauranon (a fortress just east of Nisibis) in 542 before returning to Italy. The situation in Italy deteriorated and Belisarius was recalled to Constantinople in 548, probably to retire but in 559 he (unexpectedly) defeated an invasion of Bulgar Huns.

In 562 Belisarius was prosecuted for participating in a conspiracy against Justinian I. Found guilty, he was imprisoned, but pardoned and released in July the following year (John Malalas, *Chronicle* 562–63). The story of his blinding as a punishment in 562 seems to have been invented by John Tzetzes (*Chiliades* 3.25) – no contemporary source mentions it, notably not Procopius, who surely would have done so if it had happened. Belisarius died in March 565; Justinian I died that November.

Herulians in Carthage (4.14.12); they shared the Arian faith with the Vandals and would join the revolt in 536. Procopius explains at length (6.14.1–45) that the Heruli originally came from north of the Danube River, but entered into an alliance early in Justinian I's reign.

Pharas maintained a vigilant siege of Gelimer at the foot of Mount Pappas and did not allow any supplies to reach the Vandal king, or for him to escape further. According to Procopius (4.4.33–41), Gelimer had hoped to flee to the court of the Visigoth ruler Theudis in Spain. He had given charge of his entire treasury to his scribe Boniface, who was instructed to lay at harbour at Hippo Regius and sail to Spain if things were going badly for Gelimer. After the battle of Tricamarum, Boniface had hoisted sail, but the winds were against him and he remained in Hippo Regius harbour. Taking the thwarting of his attempts to leave as a sign, he eventually decided to hand over the Vandal treasury to Belisarius.

Belisarius returned to Carthage, sent the Vandal prisoners to Constantinople and sent forces to recover for the empire other territories controlled by the Vandals, so complete was the destruction of their authority. He sent Cyril to Sardinia, carrying with him Tzazon's decapitated head as proof of his death (4.5.2–4). Some of Cyril's troops were also posted to Corsica. John the Armenian was sent with an infantry force to Caesarea (modern-day Cherchell, Algeria), 30 days' march from Carthage (4.5.5). This force was usually commanded by Belisarius himself, suggesting its elite quality and probably composed of his *bucellarii*. Another John (one of his guardsmen) was sent towards Gadira (modern-day Cádiz, Spain), situated on the Strait of Gibraltar. There was a fort there called Septem (or Septem Fratrem, near Abyla, the modern-day autonomous Spanish city of Ceuta, North Africa),

Gelimer was a great-grandson of the founder of the Vandal Empire, Gizeric (Procopius 3.9.6–9). As the younger brother of Tarasmundus, Gelimer had a strong claim to the throne, being the second-eldest male heir. In 530, Gelimer usurped the throne from his cousin, Hilderic – the reasons are unclear but probably relate more to Hilderic's defeat by the Berbers (3.9.3) than to his religious toleration (3.9.1) or his friendship with the emperors Justin I and Justinian I. Hilderic was also elderly and childless, so Gelimer would have succeeded anyway, although Gelimer accused Hilderic of plotting to change Gizeric's succession laws (3.9.20–26).

Military prowess was important to the Vandals and Hilderic was considered 'a weakling and did not wish this thing even to come to his ears' (3.9.1). By contrast, Gelimer was the best warrior of his generation, but also cunning and base and 'well versed in undertaking revolutionary enterprises and laying hold upon the money of others' (at least according to Procopius, 3.9.7). In terms of the qualities which were respected

by the Vandals, however, it seems to have been Gelimer's military prowess that was most respected (and contrasted most strongly with Hilderic) and he had support for seizing the throne (9.3.8) although there were revolts in Sardinia and Tripolis. The seemingly large number of Vandals who sought sanctuary in Carthage and later Hippo Regius may reflect opposition to Gelimer's rule, but it is difficult to be certain; many were Arians who should have supported Gelimer.

Defeated, Gelimer fled to Mount Pappas with his wife and family; their presence there is not mentioned by Procopius but is in other sources. He eventually surrendered; taken to Constantinople and paraded in triumph with his wife (John Malalas, *Chronicle* 18.81), he was retired to Galatia with an imperial pension. He was known to have laughed at his predicament (Procopius, 4.7.14–16), but this conduct was long misunderstood. Participating in Belisarius' triumph, he is meant to have remarked 'Vanity of vanities, all is vanity' (4.9.11).

so called because there were seven hills there (3.1.4–6, 4.5.6). Apollinaris, an Italian living in Libya, was sent to the islands of Ebusa (Ibiza), Majorica (Mallorca) and Minorica (Menorca) (4.5.7–8). A supporter of Hilderic, Apollinaris had come to Constantinople when Hilderic was deposed and joined Belisarius' expedition against Gelimer. He had 'proved himself a brave man in this war and most of all at Tricamarum' (4.5.9). Belisarius also sent an expedition to Tripolis, a city commanded by Pudentius and Tattimuth. Pudentius had rebelled against Gelimer (3.10.23) and Justinian I had sent Tattimuth to him although with a small force (3.10.24). Troops were also sent to Lilybaeum in Sicily although this settlement had been retaken by the Ostrogoths (3.8.13); this expedition was repulsed (4.5.11).

Meanwhile, Pharas attempted to scale Mount Pappas, but was pushed back by the Berbers (4.6.1–3). The siege was, however, biting hard on the Vandals. Procopius accuses the Vandals of being the most luxurious race, used to bathing, leisure and soft living (4.6.5–9), but now they were starving and suffering greatly. Pharas wrote to Gelimer, suggesting it would be better to throw himself on the mercy of the Byzantine emperor (4.6.15–26). Although Procopius quotes this letter at length, the contents seem unlikely; Pharas even claims, at the outset of the relatively lengthy letter, that he was not accustomed to, or skilful in, writing letters (4.6.15). After three months (therefore in March 524), the condition of Gelimer and his followers was such that he finally wrote to Pharas, offering to surrender if he received assurances of his safety (4.7.9). Pharas informed Belisarius, who was overjoyed. He sent Cyprian to Mount Pappas to deliver his oath to Gelimer, who took this and proceeded to Carthage; Belisarius wrote to the emperor, asking to send Gelimer to Constantinople (4.7.17).

The Edough massif reaches its highest point near the modern-day city of Annaba, Algeria (ancient Hippo Regius). This is one of the candidates for Mount Pappas (or Mount Papua), the precipitous mountain where Gelimer and his few remaining followers took refuge with the Berbers after his defeat at the battle of Tricamarum. Procopius' account (4.4.26–27) tells of a pursuit of the Vandals to Hippo Regius (ten days from Carthage), so Mount Pappas being nearby suits his account. The Berber city of Medeos on the side of the mountain (or any mountain) defies identification. (Jalel l'Apiculteur/Wikimedia/ CC BY-SA 3.0)

This was essentially the end of Belisarius' Vandalic War, prosecuted with remarkable skill and alacrity, and which met with even greater success than could have been hoped for. Procopius ends his account with a summation of the greatness (and unexpected nature) of Belisarius' achievements (4.7.18–21), stating that those things which seemed impossible, but which were nonetheless achieved, were worthy of wonder. Gelimer, the fourth descendant of Gizeric, and with a Vandal kingdom at the 'height of its wealth and military strength, were completely undone in so short a time by five thousand men coming in as invaders and having not a place to cast anchor' (4.7.20).

The ruins of Hippo Regius. The city had been taken by a Vandal siege in 430/31, but remained an important centre. After their defeat at the battle of Tricamarum, many Vandals retreated to Hippo Regius to take refuge and seek sanctuary in its churches. (Dan Sloan/Wikimedia/ CC BY-SA 2.0)

The Bagradas River and Scalae Veteres

AD 536

BACKGROUND TO BATTLE

After the surrender of Gelimer, events took the most remarkably Byzantine turn. Some of Belisarius' officers slandered their general (Procopius blames envy – 4.8.1), writing secretly to the emperor to accuse Belisarius of attempting to set up his own empire in North Africa. Procopius is adamant that there were no grounds for this accusation whatsoever (4.8.2; *Anecdota* 18.9). Justinian I sent the commander Solomon, bearer of the news of Belisarius' victory at the battle of Ad Decimum, back to North Africa to take over Belisarius' command. Belisarius was told that he could convey Gelimer to Constantinople in person, or stay in North Africa and Solomon could bring Gelimer back. This was a test of Belisarius' intentions, but Belisarius (having captured one of the accusers' letters) was aware of the accusations against him and chose to return to Constantinople so that he could clear his name of suspicion (4.8.5–8).

Almost as soon as Belisarius had left, Solomon began to lose control of the situation in North Africa. The Berbers began to revolt and worse problems were soon to follow. Some of the events which led to this situation we learn about only in the *Anecdota* – in which Procopius levels the accusation against Justinian I of plundering the provinces, of religious persecutions of Arian Christians, and of failing to pay the soldiers, which led to their mutiny:

> And the reason for this was that immediately after the defeat of the Vandals, Justinian not only did not concern himself with strengthening his dominion over the country, and not only did he not make provision that the safeguarding of its

wealth should rest securely in the good-will of its inhabitants, but straightway he summoned Belisarius to return home without the least delay, laying against him an utterly unjustified accusation of tyranny, to the end that thereafter, administering Libya with full licence, he might swallow it up and thus make plunder of the whole of it. At any rate he immediately sent out assessors of the land and imposed certain most cruel taxes which had not existed before. And he laid hold of the estates, whichever were best. And he excluded the Arians from the sacraments which they observed. Also he was tardy in the payment of his military forces, and in other ways became a grievance to the soldiers. From these causes arose the insurrections which resulted in great destruction. (Procopius, *Anecdota* 18.9–11)

Procopius' judgement on some of these matters in the *History of the Wars* is nowhere near as harsh, however. Of the tax assessors (Tryphon and Eustratius) sent by Justinian I, all he tells us is that they assessed 'the taxes for the Libyans each according to his proportion. But these men seemed to the Libyans neither moderate nor endurable' (4.8.25). Procopius also claimed that the revolt of the Berbers was 'for no good reason' (4.8.9).

Upon Belisarius' arrival in Constantinople with Gelimer, he was granted great honours and offered the highly unusual (and prestigious) honour of a triumph. The last non-imperial figure to hold a triumph was Marcus Vispanius Agrippa, granted a triumph after the battle of Actium in 31 BC, more than 500 years before (not quite the 600 years Procopius claims – 4.9.2). Belisarius walked in triumph in the Hippodrome in Constantinople and paraded the captured wealth of the Vandals as well as Gelimer and his family (4.9.3–13). Gelimer was given money and lands in Galatia, although he was unwilling to convert from his Arian faith and therefore not given any role in Byzantine society (had he converted, he probably would have been). By contrast, Gregory of Tours (*Historia Francorum* 2.3) states that Gilderic was broken in battle by the Romans and ended his life and reign at the same moment.

Back in Libya, Solomon continued to lose control of the situation. Aïgan, the Hun commander, and Rufinus the Thracian were killed, trapped with only

The hippodrome at Carthage is shown in this 6th-century mosaic, now in the Musée National Du Bardo, Tunis, Tunisia. When the soldiers in Carthage mutinied, they gathered in the Hippodrome and 'insulted Solomon and the other commanders without restraint' (4.14.31). Theodorus the Cappadocian was sent by Solomon to quell the mutineers, but ended up being acclaimed as their leader. From the hippodrome they marched on the palace and Solomon only barely made his escape to Belisarius. (DEA/ ARCHIVIO J. LANGE/Getty Images)

One of the peaks of the Aures Mountain Range in Belezma National Park, Algeria. After fleeing Byzantine service, 400 Vandal cavalry landed back in North Africa and proceeded to Mount Aurasium in the Aures Mountains (4.14.18–19). From there, they were recruited into Stotzas' mutiny and met their end at the battles of the Bagradas River and Scalae Veteres. (Nemencha/Wikimedia/CC BY 1.0)

a few men, in an encounter with the Berbers. Both were *foederati* commanders who had been transferred from Belisarius' to Solomon's command. Aïgan is called a bodyguard of Belisarius and Rufinus the man who carried Belisarius' standard in battle (4.10.4–12). Learning of their deaths, Solomon immediately prepared his men to avenge their demise.

While all these disasters were happening to Solomon, Belisarius was sent to Sicily, tasked with securing the island from the Goths, which he did without difficulty (4.14.1; covered in more detail in books 5–8 of the *History of the Wars*). Staying in Syracuse into spring 536, Belisarius was on hand when the greatest crisis arose in North Africa: a mutiny among the Byzantine troops stationed there.

According to Procopius (4.14.41–17.34), following victory in the Vandalic War, the wives and daughters of the Vandals were married to Byzantine soldiers; their new spouses urged them, however, to take ownership of their previous possessions (4.14.9). Solomon claimed most of that wealth for Justinian I (a different perspective again to that presented in the *Anecdota*). This discontent was one cause of the mutiny. The other cause was religious. Within the relatively small Byzantine Army were 1,000 Arian Christians, mostly Herulians (4.14.12), and the Vandal priests (also Arians) now urged them to revolt. At Easter 536, non-orthodox Christians were barred from receiving the sacrament or from being baptized (4.14.14–15). Another factor was that the Vandals taken by Belisarius to Constantinople had been enrolled in five cavalry squadrons (4.14.17), which were sent to the East to fight against the Persians. One squadron, however, overpowered their ship's crew once they reached Lesbos and forced them to head to Libya (4.14.18–19). Upon landing, they equipped themselves and ascended Mount Aurasium (the Aures Mountains in Algeria and Tunisia). Others from the former Vandal kingdom joined them there.

On Good Friday 536, a plan to assassinate Solomon failed. Some of the mutineers therefore fled Carthage, but others remained and gathered in the Hippodrome. Solomon sent Theodorus the Cappadocian to calm them (4.14.32–33), but instead the mutineers acclaimed Theodorus as their commander and marched on the palace. Solomon escaped to the harbour with another commander, Martinus, in company with Procopius, who had stayed in Carthage (4.14.38–42); after alerting other commanders along the coast by letter, they sailed to Belisarius in Syracuse.

MAP KEY

1 At the Bagradas River, some 70km from Carthage, Stotzas draws up his 9,000 men on the plain (**A**), trusting in his superior numbers to defeat Belisarius. Stotzas himself is on the right (**B**) with the Herulians and Vandals (**C**). Opposite him, Belisarius draws up his 2,000 cavalry (**D**).

2 A strong wind begins to blow into the mutineers' faces and they begin to redeploy to their right flank to threaten Belisarius' rear.

3 In the middle of this redeployment manoeuvre, Belisarius charges (targeting the Vandals), quickly routing Stotzas' entire force. The mutineers flee towards Numidia, reaching the Plain of Boulla. Most casualties are inflicted on the Vandals.

4 At Scalae Veteres, Germanus deploys his army with the baggage wagons (**A**) in the front rank immediately behind the infantry commanded by Domnicus. The best cavalry – his *bucellarii* and perhaps *excubitores* from Constantinople – are stationed on the left (**B**) opposite Stotzas. The remaining cavalry are in three divisions on the right (**C**) commanded by Ildiger, Theodorus the Cappadocian and John the brother of Pappus (with the largest contingent). Opposite them, Stotzas

arrays his mutineers in a single mass (**D**). Stotzas positions himself on the right, surrounded by his Herulian, Vandal and other cavalry (**E**). Behind them, the Berber allies are deployed (**F**) under two leaders, Iaudas and Ortaïas, who will await the outcome of the battle before engaging.

5 Stotzas wishes to charge Germanus himself but is persuaded, instead, to charge the cavalry on the Byzantine right commanded by John. This charge is initially very successful; John's cavalry give way and Stotzas' men seize the standards of John's forces. The rout looks like it will take hold of the entire Byzantine right wing and the infantry.

6 Germanus gathers his cavalry forces from his left wing and defeats the mutineers opposite them before charging into the right flank of Stotzas' cavalry. Germanus puts himself in danger and his horse is killed. His *bucellarii* close around Germanus to protect him with their shields.

7 Ildiger and Theodorus the Cappadocian (also on the Byzantine right) rally and join in Germanus' attack and rout Stotzas' cavalry. The remainder of Stotzas' mutineers flee.

Battlefield environment

Stretching 450km from north-east Algeria to the coast of Tunisia west of Tunis, the Bagradas River (the modern-day Medjerda, Tunisia) had seen many battles fought over it. According to Procopius (4.15.12–13), the battle took place 350 *stadia* from Carthage along the river, where there was high ground on which the Vandals camped. This was the site of the unwalled city of Membresa, which neither side entered. Membresa is identified with modern-day Medjez el Bab, Tunisia, which is 75.5km from Carthage on the Bagradas, although the only significant hills nearby are at modern-day El Aroussia, Tunisia, 68km from Carthage. I have located the battle midway between the two places.

The location of Scalae Veteres remains unidentified, although it too must fall within a narrow band of possibilities. Procopius tells us (4.16.10) that Stotzas brought his army within 35 *stadia* (6.5–7.4km) of Carthage before withdrawing towards Numidia. Germanus exited the city and arrayed his army. They then 'broke their ranks and withdrew, and marched off to Numidia' (4.17.1). The next detail is not, perhaps, helpful: 'And Germanus too came there with the whole army not long afterwards, having made all preparations in the best way possible and also

bringing along many wagons for the army. And overtaking his opponents in a place which the Romans call Scalae Veteres' (4.17.2–3). This would seem to give us a long line all the way into Numidia along which to search for Scalae Veteres. Several reconstructions, however, have the battle fought at the first location 6.5km from Carthage, but this is clearly not where the battle was fought. Bury (1889: ii 145) and others accepted the location as Cellas Vatari (modern-day Faïd es Siouda, Algeria), located south-east of Theveste (modern-day Tébessa, Algeria), a hill some 325km from Carthage, which seems a better option although it implies a retreat and pursuit of some distance south-westwards from Carthage, one not suggested by the brevity of Procopius' narrative, and also not back in the direction Stotzas had traversed from the Plain of Boulla and Bulla Regia, near modern-day Jendouba, Tunisia. Another suggested location is between Madauros (modern-day M'Daourouch, Algeria) and Vasampus (modern-day Morsot, Algeria), which was on the same route along which Stotzas had proceeded to Carthage from the Plain of Boulla and Gazophyla (Gadiaufala, modern-day Ksar-Sbahi, Algeria) before that.

THE BAGRADAS RIVER

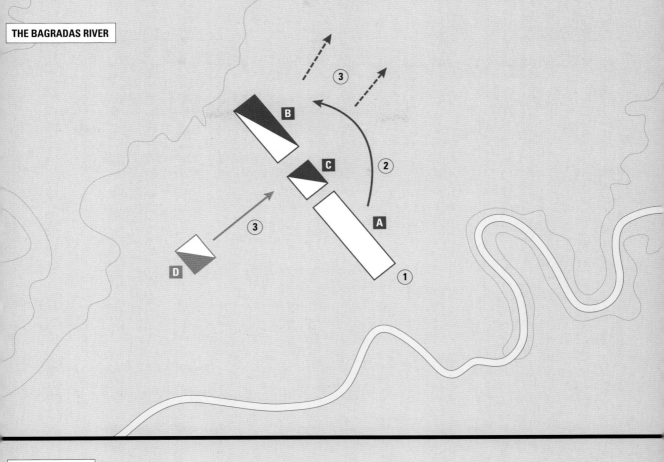

SCALAE VETERES

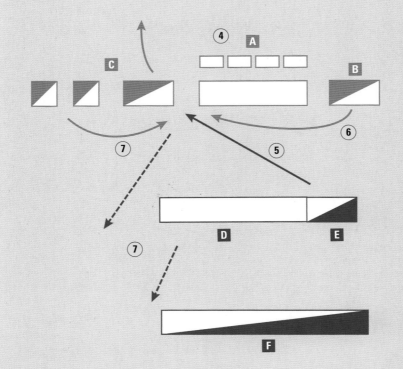

INTO COMBAT

The mutineers plundered Carthage and then gathered on the Plain of Boulla, where they elected a new commander, Theodorus the Cappadocian having not accepted his acclamation. They chose Stotzas, one of Martinus' bodyguards (4.15.1). Stotzas had a force of around 8,000 men and he marched back towards Carthage in order to take the city. He also sent word to the Vandals on Mount Aurasium (whose numbers had swelled to 1,000 men) to join him (4.15.2–4). This they willingly did. Slaves also joined his forces and together they marched on Carthage and, upon reaching it, called on Theodorus to surrender the city to them. Theodorus refused, announcing that he was guarding it for the emperor (4.15.5–7). Bury (1889: 144) adds the 1,000 Vandals to the 8,000 mutineers, bringing Stotzas' total force to 9,000 men. A messenger was sent to the mutineers: Joseph, secretary (*grammatea*) of Belisarius' *bucellarii* and a member of his household. Stotzas killed Joseph and put the city under siege (4.15.8).

In Syracuse, Belisarius selected 100 men from his *bucellarii* and, taking Solomon (and Procopius) sailed back to Carthage in a single ship, arriving at dusk (4.15.9). The besiegers expected that the city would fall to them the following morning but, learning that Belisarius had arrived, they broke the siege and retreated, such was the general's reputation. Belisarius gathered 2,000 of the troops still left in Carthage and began a pursuit (4.15.10–11). He overtook the mutineers at Membresa (identified as modern-day Medjez el Bab, Tunisia), which provides an alternative name for the battle, around 350 *stadia* from Carthage. Both armies camped and prepared for battle the following day. Belisarius' forces crossed the Bagradas River and made an entrenchment around their camp, the mutineers taking position on the high ground (probably that around El Aroussia, Tunisia, some 10km closer to Carthage). Neither side occupied Membresa, which was without walls (4.15.12–14).

Once again, Belisarius had conducted a lightning-fast march and would face a battle for which his army was outnumbered more than four to one. Marcellinus Comes (*Chronicle* 535) places the mutiny and Belisarius' response in 535, stating that Belisarius provided assistance for Solomon, who remained in overall command. This is a useful detail and it differs from the story in Procopius, in which Solomon plays little further part after fleeing to

The *Vergilius Romanus* or *Roman Vergil* is a 5th-century illustrated manuscript of the works of Vergil (now in the Biblioteca Apostolica, Vatican City, Cod. Vat. lat. 3867). The soldiers are shown in contemporary uniforms and several of the illustrations are extremely useful for uniform and equipment. Here, fol.074v shows Aeneas as a contemporary soldier complete with scale armour, round shield with boss, crested helmet and spear, as well as tunic and leggings and cross-laced boots. Although he has no bow, a quiver is shown as well. (Alonso de Mendoza/Wikimedia/Public Domain)

Belisarius in Sicily. Comes states that Belisarius restored the situation, partly through encouraging his army and partly through punishing it; a pattern which can be seen in Procopius (though he does not sum it up so pithily). Hodgkin (1896: 133) rightly observes that Belisarius must have crossed the river to reach the northern bank and confront Stotzas' forces.

Procopius tells us that 'on the day following they joined battle, the mutineers trusting in their numbers, and the troops of Belisarius despising their enemy as both without sense and without generals' (4.15.15). Belisarius wanted these sentiments to be firmly in the minds of his troops so he spoke to them (4.15.16–29), lamenting a civil conflict but one of defence and vengeance on the Romans killed by the mutineers: 'it is to avenge these their victims that we have now become enemies to those who were once most dear' (4.15.21). He reassured his men that those they fought were enemies of the state who deserved to be despised. He labelled Stotzas a tyrant ruling by fear, and stated that his men were 'handicapped in point of valour and of discipline', and so 'their defeat is ready at hand' (4.15.28). He told his men that they should hold the enemy in contempt because 'it is not by the numbers of the combatants, but by their orderly array and their bravery, that prowess in war is wont to be measured' (4.15.29).

We should be wary of the literary themes that speeches like this present; the idea of discipline prevailing over numbers had been a literary trope since the 4th century at least. The speech of Stotzas that immediately follows (4.15.30–39) is also part of a literary balancing act as well as the drama of delaying the account of the actual battle (which is brief indeed). The literary framing of battle accounts with speeches before them in a similar manner stretches back to Homer and nearly every historian since had followed a similar pattern. We must therefore take such things into consideration regarding the framing of such speeches. According to Procopius, Stotzas' speech encouraged his men, who had 'escaped our servitude to the Romans' (4.15.30). This sentiment was clearly aimed at men like the Heruli and those Vandals who had served as *foederati*. Stotzas is made to strike a fatalistic note, however, which seems unlikely in an army that outnumbered its enemy more than four to one: 'let no one of you count it unworthy to die on behalf of the freedom which you have won by your courage and your other qualities' (4.15.30). He presented his followers with two options – to become slaves to the Romans once again or to fight bravely: 'to whomsoever of you, therefore, death comes

Vergilius Romanus fol.101r shows a ruler with his bodyguard and a horse with interesting trappings. Again, we can note that even within the same unit of bodyguards, the shields are different, which perhaps suggests that shield designs had become (or reverted to) more a matter of personal taste rather than following a set design. This, however, seems to contradict the *Notitia Dignitatum*, which shows unit shield designs. This perhaps reveals a change in the century since the *Notitia Dignitatum* was compiled. (Alonso de Mendoza/Wikimedia/ Public Domain)

Vergilius Romanus fol.188v shows two armies facing one another in contemporary armour and arms. We can see a combination of spearmen and archers as well as scale armour, tunics, cloaks and a variety of shield designs (the different types of helmet are perhaps shown to distinguish between the armies). Some of the men (in the ranks behind the first?) are shown wearing less armour than those in the foreground. (Alonso de Mendoza/Wikimedia/Public Domain)

in this battle, it is plain that it will be a glorious death' (4.15.36). Stotzas considered that his force was evenly matched with Belisarius', 'for not only are the enemy greatly surpassed by us in numbers, but they will come against us without the least enthusiasm, for I think that they are praying for a share of this our freedom' (4.15.39). There is a fatalistic resignation in Stotzas' words that seems highly unlikely; his men outnumbered Belisarius' troops significantly and there should have been no reason for him to speak to men of their imminent deaths.

After the speeches of both commanders, battle was joined. A wind 'both violent and exceedingly troublesome' (Procopius, 4.15.40) began to blow into the faces of Stotzas' troops. Procopius does not offer a divine explanation of this wind as other writers might have attempted (and as he did plenty of times for phenomena in earlier battles), but nor does he present it as part of a deliberate plan undertaken by Belisarius (*if* the likely direction and timing of typical wind gusts were part of Belisarius' thinking – Belisarius was sufficiently familiar with the locale to have made it a part of his plan). Procopius does, nevertheless, state that Stotzas' troops realized that the wind could cause their missiles to be less effective and so decided to change their position, telling us that 'they therefore left their position and moved toward the [right] flank, reasoning that if the enemy should also change front, as they probably would, in order that they might not be assailed from the rear, the wind would then be in their faces' (4.15.42). In this way, Procopius summarizes a complex manoeuvre at the opening of the battle, and also seems to surmise its cause correctly.

Belisarius, seeing the enemy moving to their right flank and that they were in disorder while doing so, gave orders that the attack should begin immediately (4.15.43). Stotzas did not expect a frontal charge, instead anticipating a counter-move by Belisarius to guard against his rear being threatened. Stotzas' forces were immediately thrown into confusion by the charge and 'fled precipitately' (4.15.44), not stopping to rally until they had reached the borders of Numidia. Procopius points out that only a few of the mutineers fell in the battle, and those who did were Vandals (4.15.45), which suggests the probable target of Belisarius' charge. It is possible that Stotzas was accompanied at this battle (as he would be again later) by the Herulian cavalry and probably the Vandal cavalry too.

Belisarius did not pursue, judging that his army was too small, but allowed his men to plunder the mutineers' camp. Not a man remained, but they found many of the Vandal women who had agitated for the mutiny in the first place. Having done this, Belisarius marched back to Carthage (4.15.46–47). There he learned of a mutiny in Sicily and so he made his way quickly back to Syracuse, leaving Carthage in the charge of Ildiger and Theodorus the Cappadocian (4.15.48–49).

Having been made aware of the arrival of Stotzas, the Byzantine commanders in Numidia prepared to face him. The *foederati* commanders there were Marcellus and Cyril, with Marcellus holding the overall command, being in charge of Numidia; the cavalry were led by Barbatus, and the infantry by Terentius and Sarapis (4.15.50). Stotzas was at Gazophyla (Gadiaufala, modern-day Ksar-Sbehi, Algeria), about two days' journey from Constantina (modern-day Constantine, Algeria). Marcellus led his army against Stotzas quickly so that the mutiny would not spread to his territory. When the armies were close, however, Stotzas stepped forward and spoke, winning over the Numidian forces to his cause (4.15.53–59). The Roman commanders withdrew to Gazophyla and claimed sanctuary. Stotzas guaranteed their safety, but then killed them all when they surrendered to him.

Justinian I therefore sent his nephew Germanus at the head of a small force, with Symmachus leading the cavalry and Domnicus the infantry (4.16.1–2) to complete the suppression of the mutiny. Unfortunately, the troops assigned to Germanus were either in Carthage or had already deserted and allied with Stotzas. Germanus, therefore, began to make amends to the army and promised to right the wrongs they had suffered, claiming he had the authority of the emperor to do so (4.16.4). When the mutineers heard of this, they began to desert Stotzas. Germanus welcomed these men and even paid them for the time they were enrolled against the emperor. Learning of this, large numbers of mutineers began to march towards Carthage (4.15.5–6). When Germanus judged that the numbers he had won over matched those still under Stotzas' command, he prepared for battle.

Stotzas also wanted a decisive conflict as soon as possible to mitigate the loss of any more of his troops. He therefore marched on Carthage and got to within 35 *stadia* (6.5–7.4km) of the city (4.16.8–10). Germanus arrayed his army and marched out. After Germanus made a speech that fired his troops with enthusiasm (4.16.12–24), Stotzas' forces lost heart and began to withdraw towards Numidia. Germanus pursued and overtook the enemy at Scalae Veteres (4.17.1–3); its location may be Cellas Vatari (modern-day Faïd es Siouda, Algeria), located south-east of Theveste (modern-day Tébessa, Algeria), although this implies a pursuit of some considerable distance (325km from Carthage). Another possibility is a site between Madauros (modern-day M'Daourouch, Algeria) and Vasampus (modern-day Morsot, Algeria), which was on the same

Vergilius Romanus fol.163r shows a hunting scene, but, as noted elsewhere, the (contemporary) equipment – down to the quiver – is exactly the same as was used in warfare. Shields, spears and bows could obviously be of great benefit in a hunting context and such practices had long been considered a way of remaining in practice without the need for military drill. Cloaks and decorated tunics and leggings are especially well shown here. (Alonso de Mendoza/ Wikimedia/Public Domain)

The destruction of Stotzas at Scalae Veteres

Byzantine view: From within the ranks on the Byzantine left at the battle of Scalae Veteres, Stotzas has led a charge by his 1,000 Herulian mutineers, 1,000 Vandals and other cavalry, straight towards the right flank of the Byzantine army against the commander John the brother of Pappus. The mutineers have drawn up in a single dense formation and Stotzas' initial charge (with perhaps 2,500 men) has been successful and the mutineers and Vandals have taken John's standard, his men breaking before the enemy onslaught. Germanus, however, surrounded by his *bucellarii* and other heavily armoured cavalry, has ridden from the Byzantine left flank and charged into the right flank of the engaged mutineer and Vandal cavalry. Germanus rides directly into danger, but his *bucellarii* protect him with their shields.

Vandal view: Stotzas has led the mutineer and Vandal cavalry in a charge towards the cavalry of the Byzantine right wing, ignoring the Byzantine infantry drawn up with their backs to the baggage wagons in the centre. The 2,000 Byzantine cavalry on the right commanded by John the brother of Pappus and two others has broken when Germanus, at the head of his 500 *bucellarii* and 500 other heavy cavalry, arrives, charging directly into the right flank of the Vandals and other cavalry accompanying Stotzas. Germanus has put himself into danger and is surrounded by Vandal and mutineer cavalry, but his *bucellarii* have protected him with their shields as the Vandals attack him with their spears and swords. Mutineers and Romans are identically equipped and, even though Germanus' men cry out his name as their watchword, men inevitably find themselves fighting their former comrades.

route along which Stotzas proceeded to Carthage from the Plain of Boulla and Gazophyla and slightly closer to Carthage (some 280km).

Germanus placed his baggage wagons in the front rank, with the infantry in front of them under the command of Domnicus (4.17.4). The best of his cavalry and those brought from Constantinople were stationed on the left, the remaining cavalry on the right in three separate *lochoi* (divisions – 4.17.5). Two of these were commanded by Ildiger and Theodorus the Cappadocian while the third division, the largest, was led by John the brother of Pappus, and three other (unnamed) commanders. Stotzas arrayed his mutineers opposite them, not in any order but scattered 'more in the manner of barbarians' (4.17.7). Behind them, the Berbers were arrayed under a number of leaders, only two of whom are named: Iaudas and Ortaïas. Many of the Berbers, however, had already promised to desert to Germanus at the time of the fight (4.17.9). Germanus did not entirely trust their promises and the Berbers arrayed themselves behind, much like the situation Procopius describes for the Huns at the battle of Tricamarum, waiting to see the outcome of the fighting before deciding which side to support (4.7.10–11).

The two armies came close to each other and, seeing Germanus' standard, Stotzas encouraged his men to charge towards it (4.17.13). It is therefore likely that Stotzas had all his cavalry with him, including his Vandals. He was probably deployed on the right, prompting Germanus to deploy his best cavalry opposite Stotzas on his own left. The Herulians arrayed around Stotzas prevented this move, however, thinking that if they were repulsed the entire mutineer cause would be ruined (4.17.14–15). Stotzas therefore led his men against John on the opposite right wing. The cavalry around John broke and fled, giving up their standards to the mutineers. This rout looked like spreading to the remainder of the right wing and the infantry, but Germanus led his troops (presumably his *bucellarii*) forward and turned the tide (4.17.18). He defeated the mutineers opposite him before turning to charge the flank of Stotzas. He was joined by Ildiger and Theodorus the Cappadocian (on the right wing); as the mutineers were pushed back, it was their turn to flee.

Procopius makes an excellent point at this juncture on the nature of civil conflict: 'neither side could be distinguished either by their own comrades or by their opponents. For all used one language and the same equipment of arms, and they differed neither in figure nor in dress nor in any other thing whatever' (4.17.21). In order to be able to identify his own troops, Germanus had issued a watchword (his name); despite this, one of the enemy got close enough to kill Germanus' horse, although he was defended by his *bucellarii*, who closed around him and allowed him to mount another horse (4.17.22–23). Stotzas managed to escape but Germanus led his men straight towards the enemy camp. Capturing it after a brief struggle with the men left to guard it, Germanus took the camp, but his men immediately fell to plundering it. The Berbers meanwhile had seen the way the battle was turning out and were pursuing the fleeing mutineers and plundering their camp too. Stotzas, however, unaware of their perfidy, had attempted to persuade the Berber force to renew the attack (4.17.32). Forced to escape further, and with many of his men surrendering to Germanus' troops, Stotzas fled with only 100 men, mostly Vandals, into Mauretania where he stayed. The mutiny in North Africa was over, however.

Analysis

BYZANTINE EFFECTIVENESS

Averil Cameron calls the Vandalic War Belisarius' 'greatest success' (1985: 171); and despite the campaign being Justinian I's idea, and one he pursued despite fierce opposition, it was indeed Belisarius who made all the difference. Without his energy and planning the campaigns would not have been so successful or so rapidly undertaken. His arrival, rapid march, fighting two decisive battles, and retaking and fortifying Carthage in 533 all took place within the space of a few months – the battles of Ad Decimum and Tricamarum were fought only three months apart and he had left Constantinople in late June; the whole war was waged in six months. The thing which took most time was the besieging and surrender of Gelimer, not coming until March 534. When Belisarius was not on the scene (as happened because of jealousy and rivalry in 534), things quickly fell apart and he needed to return to quell the mutiny of troops in 536. This he did in a lightning-fast return, winning victory at the battle of the Bagradas River. Procopius does mention Belisarius' qualities but he also, at times, plays them down. His overall judgement of the Vandal campaigns was that the victories appeared impossible to achieve, but that Gelimer, at the height of Vandal power and wealth, was brought down in a very short time by only 'five thousand men coming in as invaders and having not a place to cast anchor' (4.7.20). This point (ignoring the 10,000 infantry) emphasizes that Belisarius' victories in North Africa were achieved by his cavalry alone.

As many of Procopius' details tell us, the troops Belisarius had were no better than those that had come before or which were available to other commanders – and he had only 15,000 men in total, with just 5,000 cavalry. He did, however, have a remarkable skill at disciplining his army and keeping those men together as a cohesive, disciplined fighting unit. It was the success at Tricamarum which (ironically) ultimately destroyed that cohesion. Belisarius

This 6th-century Byzantine hunting mosaic shows a horseman thrusting a spear, one-handed and underhand. The mosaic originated in a church in Kissufim, Negev; it is now in the Israel Museum, Jerusalem. (www. BibleLandPictures.com/Alamy Stock Photo)

also had very capable subordinates, especially his cavalry commander John, who was instrumental at both Ad Decimum and Tricamarum. His death (Procopius goes into detail about it) was a tremendous loss indeed. In these victories it was the *bucellarii* who were entrusted with the lion's share of the work. Other commanders were less capable and perfidious, consumed by petty jealousy as the secret accusations against Belisarius of treason show. Solomon, appointed to succeed Belisarius in Africa, had very little success and not the same energy or capability to face the threats that emerged. In this he was hamstrung by imperial policy – something Procopius also highlights (*Anecdota* 18.9) – aimed at amassing as much wealth as possible.

Dating from 578, this Byzantine mosaic, from a church in Kissufim, Negev, and now held in the Israel Museum, Jerusalem, shows a bear hunt. We can see the long tunic and sword on a baldric as well as the use (and utility) of a shield even when hunting. The long tunic and leggings look very similar to those depicted in mosaics from Carthage. (Hemis/Alamy Stock Photo)

Belisarius was also highly capable of using his *foederati* effectively. The Huns at the battle of Ad Decimum did exactly what was needed of them and other *foederati* occupied the wings at the battle of Tricamarum. The Heruli under Pharas were clearly trusted to besiege Gelimer on Mount Pappas even though they later mutinied when Belisarius had departed. Belisarius' tactics also showed he had learned from the tactics of his *foederati*; the feigned retreats of John's cavalry charges in the centre at Tricamarum, designed to lure the Vandals into pursuing, were a ploy he had probably learned from the Huns.

The most remarkable aspect of the Vandalic War in terms of battle tactics, however, is not the war of rapid manoeuvre that was clearly part of Belisarius' success, but the fact that all of the military victories were achieved by cavalry charges – whether mounted by light cavalry (putting the Huns at Ad Decimum into that category) or heavy cavalry (such as those of John at Ad Decimum), and the charge of all the cavalry, outnumbered, at Gelimer's force. At the battles of the Bagradas River and Scalae Veteres it was cavalry charges that decided the battle – and relatively quickly: Germanus' came later than it might have if Belisarius had been in command. Only at the battle of Tricamarum was the cavalry charge less effective when, twice, Tzazon refused to take the bait of a feigned retreat; but again a mass cavalry charge decided the battle when Tzazon was felled and the remainder of the Vandal army fled.

VANDAL EFFECTIVENESS

When Belisarius invaded Vandal North Africa, the Vandal Empire was at the height of its wealth and power and at almost its greatest extent. The Byzantine fear of whether a Vandal navy might ambush them reflects the fact that Vandal navies threatened most of the western Mediterranean. It is clear that the Vandals outnumbered Belisarius massively – 80,000 men to Belisarius' 15,000. Even if we reduce that number to a more reasonable 32,000, the Vandals still had the advantage – and their men all served as cavalry. That immense power was, however, a mirage. Belisarius must have seen through the mirage; otherwise his decisive actions outnumbered perhaps by up to four to one seem foolhardy. At the battle of the Bagradas River he was again outnumbered four to one, choosing to attack 8,000 mutineers (perhaps 9,000) with only 2,000 men of his own. One aspect of the rapid and complete defeat of the Vandals is, therefore, the fragility of their power and their morale – they outnumbered the invading force massively: Procopius tells us their 80,000 cavalry faced only 5,000 Roman cavalry (often piecemeal where individual Roman contingents were similarly outnumbered) and still they lost. The Vandals hardly encountered Belisarius' 10,000 infantry. Despite this numerical superiority and a series of advantages such as Gelimer's trap to surround the advancing Romans at the battle of Ad Decimum, they were unable to defeat this small force.

Part of this was down to poor timing on the part of Ammatas and the defeat of Gibamundus at Ad Decimum, but it was also something more intangible. If Procopius' account is to believed, Gelimer and the Vandals' lamenting the death of Ammatas is what led to their complete rout at Ad Decimum when Belisarius advanced with his entire cavalry force. Bury called Gelimer a man of 'sentimental temperament' and claimed that the death of his brother 'completely unmanned' him (1889: 135); it is hard to understand Gelimer's actions in any other way. Gelimer's force still outnumbered Belisarius' and he should still have won, but his men broke at the first charge. It is true that he may have considered he had won the day's engagement when the *foederati* withdrew. Despite still outnumbering the invaders, the rest of the Vandals apparently fled without much of a fight; the 800 casualties sustained at Tricamarum (4.3.18) certainly does not represent a high or calamitous loss of life. Bury, however, is harsher in his criticism, calling Gelimer weak and incompetent: 'he had no idea of using to advantage his great numerical preponderance in cavalry' (1889: 137). At Tricamarum, too, the flight of the Vandals followed the defeat of Tzazon, their most successful general, who had put up a staunch resistance. The same thing would happen at the battle of the Bagradas River.

The immediate and precipitate flight of the Vandal armies is also shocking – they were only able to rally at a great distance from their reversals and, after the battle of Tricamarum, Gelimer with only a few followers headed far away to Mount Pappas. Many of the remaining Vandals sought sanctuary, first in Carthage and then elsewhere such as Hippo Regius, and they surrendered to Belisarius. Unlike Stotzas subsequently, Belisarius honoured those terms. The Vandals' very act of seeking sanctuary may also suggest that there was a large degree of opposition to Gelimer, with individuals looking for an opportunity to defect; the fact Carthage was not betrayed back to Gelimer suggests the same thing and there are other suggestions that opposition to his rule was rife among the Vandals themselves, not just their subjects.

At the same time, however – and despite Procopius' comment on the vast loss of life in the *Anecdota* – the power of the Vandals was not utterly lost or destroyed; there were still enough Vandal warriors to provide Justinian I with 2,000 cavalry, and more men remained able to join Stotzas' mutiny. The casualties reported are not excessive and many of the Vandals lived to fight another day.

The only Vandal commander who seems to have had any success was Tzazon, first against Godas in Sardinia and then in putting up a successful defence in the opening stages of the battle of Tricamarum. Other Vandal commanders – Ammatas, Gibamundus and Gelimer himself – seem to have been much less capable. Bury surmised that Gelimer 'committed the most amazing mistakes, which his enemies could not have foreseen' (1889: 128), although this judgement suggests that Belisarius was supremely lucky in addition to his other qualities.

The Berber allies of the Vandals were effective – they had proven themselves problematic to the Vandals themselves and in raids against various cities and, after the collapse of Byzantine control of North Africa, they would become the power to be reckoned with and would revolt again during 544–48 and again in 563 (John Malalas, *Chronicle* 563). They were also, however, susceptible to changing sides; parallels can be drawn with the Huns' behaviour at the battle of the Bagradas River and the Berbers' conduct at the battle of Scalae Veteres.

Aftermath

According to Procopius (*Anecdota* 18.1–9), the Vandalic War cost five million lives (18.8) and this is part of the vast toll of those who perished under Justinian I; Procopius' total is a 'myriad myriad of myriads' or one trillion (18.4). We should be wary of exaggeration here, however, for Procopius' intention in the *Anecdota* was to blacken Justinian I's name.

Belisarius had no time to rest on his laurels; by the time of Germanus' victory at the battle of Scalae Veteres in 536 he had already taken Sicily from the Ostrogoths and had invaded Italy. He would go on to re-conquer Naples and Rome before the year was out (taking Rome on 9 December). Times were unsettled, however, and Belisarius' fortunes in Italy were varied: in 540 he captured Ravenna and the Ostrogoth king, Witigis, but he had been offered the throne of Italy and this brought his loyalty (again) under suspicion. As a result, Belisarius was recalled to Constantinople and then sent to fight against the

The reverse on a cast of a gold medallion of Justinian I, issued in 534 to commemorate his victory over the Vandals. Justinian I, mounted, wearing a muscled cuirass, *pteruges* and a *toupha* feathered crown and carrying a lance, is led by an angel with the palm of victory and a military standard. He was similarly depicted on the victory column erected in Constantinople. The legend declares *Salvus et Gloria Romanorum*: 'Salvation and Glory of the Romans'. Minted in Constantinople (CONOB), the coin was found in Caesarea ad Argaeum (Mazaca, modern-day Kayeri, Turkey) in 1751, but stolen in 1831 from the Cabinet des Médailles of the Bibliothèque Nationale de France in Paris. (Granger Historical Picture Archive/Alamy Stock Photo)

Sassanian Persians once again in 541 in the Lazic War (541–62); the 'Endless Peace' of 532 had lasted less than nine years. He returned to Italy in 544 to once again rescue a situation which had deteriorated without him, but these campaigns were ultimately unsuccessful and Belisarius was replaced in 549. Also in 544, a Berber revolt occurred in North Africa and would last until 548 (Jordanes, *Romana* 384–85; Marcellinus Comes, *Chronicle* 545–47); and another occurred in 563

(John Malalas, *Chronicle* 563). A much larger and better-equipped invasion would succeed in Italy during 552–54. Despite eventual success, all the gains were lost soon after Justinian I's death in 565; his and Belisarius' efforts to regain the West were the last gasp of the Western Roman Empire, as it soon fell irrevocably to various warring factions. Belisarius retired, but was called back to command again in 559, when he defeated an invading force of Bulgar Huns and was once more hailed a hero. Jordanes' *Romana* (366–82) summarizes Belisarius' career up to 552 and is full of praise.

The Vandal Empire, which had been flourishing and seemingly all-powerful in 532, was destroyed, never to be revived – and that total collapse took barely six months. The loss of life and destabilization would have long-lasting effects. If we believe the accusations of Procopius, the whole of North Africa was bled dry. The entire region would fall to Arabic conquests in the following century: Tunisia was invaded in 647 and Morocco in 682; the Strait of Gibraltar was crossed and the Iberian Peninsula invaded in 711.

Perhaps because of the eventual failure of Justinian I's conquests, they were quickly overshadowed, and Belisarius' truly remarkable accomplishments seem to have been all but forgotten, especially by some Byzantine writers. The peculiar, late invention of Belisarius' blinding was latched onto to a disproportionate degree in comparison with what he had achieved. His campaigns were lightning fast, often with very limited resources and support, but his immense accomplishments belied the meagre resources assigned to him: his decisive actions were often delivered by his outnumbered *bucellarii*. He often seems to have embraced such odds, if not actually sought them out, gladly marching against Gelimer's 80,000 men with only 15,000 troops and then happily pursuing Stotzas' 8,000-strong forces with only 2,000 men of his own. In 559 he would lead only 300 men (and an army of civilians and peasants) to victory at Melantias.

Belisarius was by far and away the best general of his generation; it is not for nothing that he is known as the last Roman or, in Gibbon's phrase, 'the Africanus of new Rome' (1788: 621). Yet a neglect of Belisarius began soon after his death and has continued. Agathias opened his late-6th-century *Histories* stating that his own work would continue Procopius' (Preface 24); he then credited the war fought against Gelimer and the subjugation of Carthage and Africa to Justinian I (Belisarius is not named). Agathias also summarizes the mutiny in Africa and the destruction of Stotzas, but again Belisarius is omitted. When he recounts the final victory of Belisarius in 559, however, Agathias does write of him being refilled with youthful vigour, like Leonidas (because he led 300 men), and wining a glory as great as that against the Vandals (*Histories* 5.15.8). Following Agathias, John of Nikiû, writing in Egypt at the end of the 7th century, records in his *Chronicle* (92.19–20) that

Obverse of the Justinian I medallion commemorating his victory over the Vandals. Justinian I took the titles of *Vandalicus* and *Africanus* in November 533 (*Institutes* Proemium), before the battle of Tricamarum had been fought. Here, he is shown in the same military dress as on the reverse. The legend reads 'DNJustinianusPPAug' (*Dominus Noster Justinianus Perpetuus Augustus*: 'Our Lord Justinian, Eternal Augustus'. On earlier coinage 'PP' stood for *Pater Patriae* ('Father of the Country'), but this had come to mean 'Perpetual' under 4th- and 5th-century Roman rulers. With the exception of Procopius, other historians soon gave all credit for the Vandal victory to Justinian I himself. It was clearly the emperor's initiative, although the expedition appears to have been massively under-resourced. The fact that Belisarius achieved such spectacular results with fewer men and ships than should have been necessary makes his accomplishments all the more remarkable. (Granger Historical Picture Archive/ Alamy Stock Photo)

it was Justinian I who conquered the Vandals and that Agathias had carefully recorded these victories (he names Agathias as his source before he mentions Procopius, and summarizes nothing of the latter's work).

The Vandals' own rapid conquests and establishment of a vast North African and Mediterranean empire were remarkable in themselves. The empire had, however, fallen apart in record time – Carthage was recaptured 96 years after its capture by the Vandals in 439 (Marcellinus Comes *Chronicle* 534). For a long time the only thing the Vandals were remembered for was their name, a term conveying wanton destruction and disrespect for culture. This, of course, came into being at a time when Vandal culture itself was misunderstood and disrespected and, as North African remains attest, they often wrought much less destruction than their reputation suggests. We should also remember that they were heretic Arian Christians attacking orthodox Nicene Christians, and it is the latter whose accounts survive.

One aspect of Belisarius' victories against the Vandals that would have a lasting impact was the increasing dependence of armies upon cavalry. By the end of the 6th century and the writing of Maurice's *Strategikon*, the expectation was that the majority of the Byzantine field army would be composed of cavalry. Perhaps this was an (unexpected and unrecognized) influence of the Vandals, whose own armies were composed of cavalry-only forces. This development was aided immensely by the arrival of the stirrup by the end of the 6th century – perhaps via the Turkish Avars (although that subject is still much debated). What Belisarius' victories in North Africa exhibited especially, and perhaps more than any other Late Roman candidate, was the decisive use of cavalry, both heavy and light, often without the involvement of infantry. What is more, Belisarius' tactics embraced and used horse-archery and heavy *bucellarii* charges differently and to great effect.

BIBLIOGRAPHY

Sources

Our major, sometimes sole, source for the Vandalic War is the contemporary historian **Procopius of Caesarea** (*c*.500–*c*.570). Procopius' surviving works – the eight books of the *History of the Wars* (*Hyper ton Polemon Logoi*, literally 'Words on the Wars'), *On Buildings*, and *Anecdota* (or *Secret History*) – each make important points about the history of the era. The *History of the Wars* was written before 545, although the eighth book was added later to continue the narrative to 551. Books 1 and 2 cover the Persian Wars, books 3 and 4 the Vandalic War and the remaining four books the Gothic Wars. The scandalous and vicious content of the *Anecdota* is markedly different from the perspective in the *History of the Wars*, launching scathing attacks on Justinian I, Theodora, Belisarius and Antonina (Belisarius' wife) that are entirely missing from Procopius' other works. Procopius was a legal adviser (*assessor*) to Belisarius as *magister militum* in 527 and became his secretary (he tells us he was Belisarius' advisor (*paredron* – 3.14.3). He accompanied Belisarius to North Africa in 533 and remained there after Belisarius' successes. He is therefore an invaluable eyewitness to Belisarius' campaigns, and his close relationship to his patron gave him insights few historians have had into a military campaign. He stayed in Carthage until 536 when he joined Belisarius once more for the latter's campaign to reclaim Italy from the Goths in 537. After that campaign, the relationship between the two men deteriorated.

Procopius seems a trustworthy and detailed source, although his varying perspectives allow us to question his reliability. In many cases, however, alternative sources only offer us the briefest of accounts and our ability to cross-reference and corroborate Procopius' view of events is often quite limited. The late-6th-century historian **Agathias**, who wrote a continuation of Procopius, can be used and his summary of events up to when his own account starts does, indeed, accord with Procopius'. **John of Nikiû** used Agathias as his source in his late-7th-century *Chronicle*.

We can also use the treatise that has come down to us as *Strategikon* of the Byzantine emperor **Maurice**, probably written in the late 6th century in 11 books. It is the most important of the Byzantine military handbooks

and provides us with details of formations and tactics of both Byzantine forces and the enemies they faced. It is very useful for earlier periods because it was, in part, a compilation of earlier treatises. At some point in the manuscript tradition, a twelfth book was added that included **Urbicius**' *Epitedeuma*, a treatise written for Anastasius in the late 5th or early 6th centuries and an infantry treatise. This infantry handbook seems to have been written during the reign of Justinian I (and also includes advice on cavalry tactics) and therefore has direct relevance to the campaigns of the 530s. The *Anonymous Byzantine Treatise on Strategy* was also written during Justinian I's reign.

A page from the *Codex Argenteus*, a 6th-century manuscript containing the translation of the Bible into Gothic first made in the 4th century by bishop Ulfilas (or Ulphilas, Orphila or Wulfila). Ulfilas was an Arian Christian and the Goths and Vandals adhered to the Arian faith long after others had abandoned it. Many of the clashes of the 4th, 5th and 6th centuries arose, in part, due to conflicts between the Arian and Nicene faiths. Merrills and Miles argue (2014: 237) that Justinian I cast the conquest of North Africa as a crusade to unite orthodox Romano-Africans with their church. (World History Archive/Alamy Stock Photo)

Other sources that touch on this era do so lightly. The *Getica* or *History of the Goths* of **Jordanes**, who was writing in 551, comes to a close with the year 542 and mentions that Justinian had won a triumph over the Vandals (307). Similarly, his *Romana* mentions Belisarius' campaigns as recent history.

The *Variae* of the late-6th-century Italian senator **Cassiodorus** tells us of the author's grandfather's survival of the Vandal raids on Italy in the 440s and 450s. The *Chronicle* of **John Malalas**, written during the reign of Justinian I, is relevant though brief. Likewise, the *Chronicle* of **Marcellinus Comes**, written in Constantinople later in the 6th century, deals briefly with the Vandalic War. **Gregory of Tours'** late 6th century *Historia Francorum* contains some information on the Vandals although his chronology is very muddled and he clearly despises the Arian faith to which they adhered. The *Chronicon Paschale*, composed in around 630, is, however, silent on the Vandalic War. Other sources can be used on occasion such as **Isidore**'s *Gothic History*, **Sozomen**'s *Ecclesiastical History* and the abbreviation of **Zacharias Rhetor**'s (known as *The Syriac Chronicle*). The *Codex Justinianus* contains two edicts (1.27.1–2) relating specifically to pay grades in Africa in 534 and we can also use the *Novels* (or *New Constitutions*) and the *Institutes of Justinian*. The 12th-century *Chiliades* by **John Tzetzes** contains the (probably fictional) story of the blinding of Belisarius by Justinian I in the 560s, but also mentions the fate of Gelimer and Belisarius' Vandal victories.

Ancient works

Agathias, *The Histories*, trans. J.D. Frendo (1975), in *Corpus Fontium Historiae Byzantinae* vol. 2A, Series Berolinensis. Berlin: Walter de Gruyter.

Ammianus Marcellinus, *Rerum gestarum libri*, trans. C.D. Yonge (1862). London: Henry. G. Bohn.

Anonymous, *Anonymous Byzantine Treatise on Strategy*, trans. G.T. Dennis (1985), in *Three Byzantine Military Treatises*. Washington, DC: Dumbarton Oaks.

Caesar, *The Civil Wars*, trans. A.G. Peskett (1914). Two volumes. Cambridge, MA & London: Harvard University Press.

Caesar, *The Gallic War*, trans. H.J. Edwards (1917). Cambridge, MA & London: Harvard University Press.

Cassiodorus, *Variae, Letters*, trans. S.J.B. Barnish (1992). Liverpool: Liverpool University Press.

Chronicon Paschale, trans. M. & M. Whitby (1989). Liverpool: Liverpool University Press.

Gregory of Tours, *History of the Franks*, trans. E. Brehaut (1916). New York, NY: Columbia University Press.

Isidore of Seville, *History of the Kings of the Goths, Vandals, and Suevi*, trans. G. Donini & G.B. Ford (1966). Leiden: E.J. Brill.

Jerome, *Letters*, trans. W.H. Fremantle, G. Lewis & W.G. Martley (1893), in *Nicene and Post-Nicene Fathers*, Second Series, Vol. 6. Buffalo, NY: Christian Literature Publishing Co.

John Malalas, *Chronicle*, trans. E. Jeffreys, M. Jeffreys & R. Scott (1986). Melbourne: Australian Association for Byzantine Studies.

John of Nikiû, *Chronicle*, trans. R.H. Charles (1913). London: Williams & Norgate.

John Tzetzes, *Chiliades*, trans. A. Untila, G. Berkowitz et al. (2018), at https://archive.org/details/TzetzesCHILIADES

Jordanes, *Romana*, trans. P. Van Nuffelen & L. Van Hoof (2020). Liverpool: Liverpool University Press.

Jordanes, *The Gothic History*, trans. C.C. Mierow (1915). Princeton, NJ: Princeton University Press.

Justinian, *The Codex of Justinian*, trans. F.H. Blume & ed. B.W. Frier (2016). Three volumes. Cambridge: Cambridge University Press.

Justinian, *The Institutes of Justinian*, trans. J.B. Moyle (1893). Oxford: Clarendon Press.

Marcellinus Comes, *Chronicle*, trans. B. Croke (1995). Sydney: Australian Association for Byzantine Studies.

Maurice, *Strategikon*, trans. G.T. Dennis (1984). Philadelphia, PA: University of Pennsylvania Press.

Procopius, *History of the Wars*, trans. H.B. Dewing (1914–28). Five volumes. Cambridge, MA & London: Harvard University Press.

Procopius, *On Buildings*, trans. H.B. Dewing & G. Downey (1940). Cambridge, MA & London: Harvard University Press.

Procopius, *The Secret History*, trans. H.B. Dewing (1935). Cambridge, MA & London: Harvard University Press.

Sozomen, *Ecclesiastical History*, trans. E. Walford (1855). London: Henry G. Bohn.

Suda – The Suda Online http://www.cs.uky.
edu/~raphael/sol/sol-html/ (originally stoa.org).

Urbicius, *Epitedeuma*, trans. G. Greatrex, H. Elton & R.
Burgess (2005), in 'Urbicius' Epitedeuma: an
edition, translation and commentary', *Byzantinische
Zeitschrift* 98: 35–74.

Vegetius, *Epitome of Military Science*, trans. N.P. Milner
(1993). Liverpool: Liverpool University Press.

Zacharias Rhetor, *The Syriac Chronicle known as that of
Zachariah of Mitylene*, trans. F.J. Hamilton & E.W.
Brooks (1899). London: Methuen & Co.

Modern works

Atanasov, G. (2014). 'The portrait of Flavius Aetius
(390–454) from Durostorum (Silistra) inscribed on
a consular diptych from Monza', *Studia Academica
Šumenensia* 1: 7–21.

Bury, J.B. (1889). *A History of the Later Roman Empire*.
Two volumes. London & New York, NY: Macmillan
& Co.

Cameron, A. (1985). *Procopius and the Sixth Century*.
London & New York, NY: Routledge.

Delbrück, H., trans. Walter J. Renfroe, Jr. (1980). *The
Barbarian Invasions* (History of the Art of War
Vol. II). Lincoln, NE: University of Nebraska Press.
Originally published in German in 1921.

Diehl, C. (1896). *L'Afrique byzantine. Histoire de la
domination byzantine en Afrique (533–709)*. Paris:
Ernest Leroux.

Evans, J.A.S. (1996). *The Age of Justinian: The
circumstances of imperial power*. London & New
York, NY: Routledge.

Gibbon, E. (1776). *The History of the Decline and Fall of
the Roman Empire*. Volume 1. London: W. Strahan
& T. Cadell.

Gibbon, E. (1781). *The History of the Decline and Fall of
the Roman Empire*. Volume 2. London: W. Strahan
& T. Cadell.

Gibbon, E. (1781). *The History of the Decline and Fall of
the Roman Empire*. Volume 3. London: W. Strahan
& T. Cadell.

Gibbon, E. (1788). *The History of the Decline and Fall of
the Roman Empire*. Volume 4. London: W. Strahan
& T. Cadell.

Haldon, J. (2008). *The Byzantine Wars*. Stroud: The
History Press.

Heather, P. (2007). *The Fall of the Roman Empire. A New
History*. London: Pan.

Heather, P. (2018). *Rome Resurgent: War and Empire in
the Age of Justinian*. Oxford: Oxford University Press.

Hodgkin, T. (1892–96). *Italy and Her Invaders*. Two
volumes. Second Edition. Oxford: Clarendon Press.

Hughes, I. (2009). *Belisarius: The Last Roman General*.
Yardley, PA: Westholme.

Jones, A.H.M. (1964). *The Later Roman Empire 284–
602*. Two volumes. Norman, OK: University of
Oklahoma Press.

Lord Mahon (Stanhope, P., 5th Earl Stanhope) (1829).
The Life of Belisarius. London: John Murray.

Maas, M., ed. (2005). *The Cambridge Companion to the
Age of Justinian*. Cambridge: Cambridge University
Press.

MacDowall, S. (2016). *The Vandals*. Barnsley: Pen &
Sword.

Merrills, A., ed. (2016). *Vandals, Romans and Berbers:
New Perspectives on Late Antique North Africa*.
London & New York, NY: Routledge.

Merrills, A. & Miles, R. (2014). *The Vandals*. Chichester:
Wiley Blackwell.

Negin, A. & D'Amato, R. (2018). *Roman Heavy Cavalry
(1): Cataphractarii & Clibinarii, 1st Century BC–5th
Century AD*. Elite 225. Oxford: Osprey.

Negin, A. & D'Amato, R. (2020). *Roman Heavy Cavalry
(2): AD 500–1450*. Elite 235. Oxford: Osprey.

Nicholson, O., ed. (2018). *Oxford Dictionary of Late
Antiquity*. Two volumes. Oxford: Oxford University
Press.

Tissot, C.J. (1888). *Exploration scientifique de la Tunisie:
géographie comparée de la province romaine d'Afrique*.
Volume 2. Paris: Imprimerie Nationale.

Treadgold, W. (1995). *Byzantium and Its Army, 284–
1081*. Stanford, CA: Stanford University Press.

Whately, C. (2014). *Battles and Generals: Combat,
Culture, and Didacticism in Procopius' 'Wars'*. Leiden
& Boston, MA: Brill.

Whately, C. (2015). 'Some Observations on Procopius'
use of Numbers in Descriptions of Combat in *Wars*
Books 1–7', *Phoenix* 69: 394–411.

Whately, C. (2021). *Procopius on Soldiers and Military
Institutions in the Sixth-Century*. Leiden & Boston,
MA: Brill.

INDEX

References to illustrations are shown in **bold**. References to plates are shown in bold with caption pages in brackets, e.g. **66–67**, (68).

Ad Decimum, battle at 8, **9**, 22, 29–32, **33**, 34–40, 36, 42, 43, (52), 70, 72–73
  forces' strengths/dispositions 11, **12**, **13**, 14, 15–16, 17, 18, 22, 26, 32, **33**, 34, 36–37, 38, 39, 48, 52, 53, 72, 73
  tactics 18, 27–28, 32, **33**, 34, 72
Aïgan (Hunnic commander) 48, 58–59
Alani forces 4, 16, 17, **17**, 26, 27
Althias (commander) 14, 32, 38, 44, **45**, 48
Ammatas (Gelimer's brother) 8, 12, 15–16, 23, 31, 35, 39, 73
  at Ad Decimum 17, 18, 32, **33**, 36–37, 38, 43, 72
Anastasius I Dicorus (emperor) 5, **5**
Archelaus (prefect) 30, 35
Armenian forces 14, 15, 30

Bagradas River (the), battle at 57–60, 61, **61**, 62–65, 70, 73
  forces' strengths/dispositions 14, 28, 60, **61**, 72, 73
  tactics 28
Balas (Hunnic commander) 14, 44, **45**
Barbatus (commander) 44, **45**, 48, 65
Belisarius (Roman general) 4, **5**, **21**
  achievements 54, 56, 70, 75
  at Ad Decimum 27–28, 32, **33**, 34–35, 37–38, 39, 73
  at Bagradas River 28, 60, **61**, 62, 64
  at Tricamarum 14, 44, **45**, 48
  command/generalship 21, 29, 37–38, 46, 53, 63, 70: command of expedition 7, 8, 9, 10, 14, 15, 29–30, 55; and mutiny of troops 8, 70; treatment of Vandals 16, 41, 53
  in Carthage 40, 41, 42, 46, 52, 54, 70
  in Italy 28, 54, 74–75
  in Sicily 59, 63, 64–65, 74
  military career 54
  neglect of 75–76
  opposition to 57
  retirement/recall 75
Berber forces 6, 16, 17, 38, 43, 55, 56, 57, 58, 59, 60, **61**, 69, 73, 74
bodyguard cavalry (*doryphoroi*) 11, 11, 14, 21, 38, 48, 49, 54, 63
bucellarii (guard units) **11**, 15, 21, 22, 23, 40, 46, 54, 62, 71, 75, 76
  use in battle 11, **12**, **13**, 14, 18, 32, **33**, 34, 36–37, 39, 44, **45**, 48–49, **50–51**, (52), 53, 60, **61**, **66–67**, (68), 69
Byzantine army (cavalry) 7, 11, 12, **12**, 13, 14, 15, **28**
  armour/clothing 5, **12**, **13**, **14**, **17**, 24, **25**, **26**, **27**, **28**, 38, **62**, 64, 65, 71, 74, 76
  command structure 10, 21–22
  composition/strength 7, 10–11, 13, 14–15, 17, 20, 21–22, 26, 48, (52), 52, 69, 70, 72, 75
  helmets **12**, **13**, **14**, **15**, **17**, 62, 64, 65
  mutiny of troops 22, 59
  ranks/paygrades/troop types 22, 24, 26
  weapons/equipment 5, 11, **11**, **12**, **13**, 14, **14**, **16**, **17**, 24, 25, **25**, 26, 30, **38**, **39**, **62**, 63, 64, 65, **66–67**, **71**, 72, 76
Byzantine fleet/navy 8, **9**, 29–30, 30–31, **30**, 34, 35, 36, 37, 40, 41

Calonymus (admiral) 30, 35, 40, 41
Carthage, fighting for 4, 6, 8, **9**, 12, 15–16, 30,

31, **34**, 35, 37, 40, **40**, 41, 42, 43, **43**, 46, 47, 52, 53, 55, 58, **58**, 62, 69, 70, 73, 76
cataphractarii/clibanarii (heavy cavalry) 11, **12**, **13**, 14, 18, 23, 49, **50–51**, (52)
coinage, depictions on 29, **29**, **34**, **74**, **75**
Corsica, forces on 8, **9**, 54
Cyprian (commander) 14, 32, 38, 44, **45**, 48, 55
Cyril (commander) 14, 15, 22, 38, 42, 54, 65

Domnicus (commander) 60, **61**, 65, 69
Dorotheus (commander) 14, 30, 38

foederati forces 7, 10, 11, 14, 15, 22, 27, 30, 32, **33**, 34, 38–39, 40, 42, 44, **45**, 48, 59, 65, 71, 72, 73

Gelimer (Vandal king) 4, 6, 12, 15, 16, 17, 23, 29, 30, 31, 34, 35, 55, 56, 73
  at Ad Decimum 8, **9**, 18, 32, **33**, 34, 35, 36, 39–40, (52), 43
  at Carthage 8, 41, 42, 43
  at Tricamarum 6, 27, 44, **45**, 46, 47, 48, 52
  pursuit/surrender of 53–54, 55, 57, 58, 70, 72, 73
Germanus (commander) 8, 26, 28, 60, **61**, 65, **66–67**, (68), 69, 72, 74
Gibamundus (Gelimer's nephew) 16, 18, 23, 32, **33**, 36, 37, 38, 39, 43, 52, 72, 73
Giziric (Vandal king) 4, 55, 56
Godas (governor of Sardinia) 6, 22, 42, 73
Goth forces 24, 26, 27, 59
Gunthamundus (Vandal king) 4, 5

Herulian forces 14, 15, 53–54, 59, 60, **61**, 63, 64, **66–67**, (68), 69
Hilderic (Gelimer's cousin) 5–6, 16, **34**, 35, 55
Hippo Regius 8, **9**, 44, 53, 54, 55, 56, **56**, 73
Hoamer ('Achilles of the Vandals') 6, 16
Honoric (Vandal king) 4, 5
Honorius I (emperor) 11, 37
horse fitting/trappings (Byz) **5**, **12**, **13**, **14**, 24, **28**, **63**
horse fittings/trappings (Van) 7, **18**, **19**, **23**, 24
Huneric (Vandal king) 16, 37
Hunnic forces 11, 14, 15, 22, 26, 27, 32, **33**, 34, 36–37, 39, 40, 44, **45**, 46, 48, 49, 52, 58–59, 69, 72, 73

Iaudas (Berber leader) 60, **61**, 69
Ildiger (commander) 60, **61**, 65, 69
imperial guards (*excubitores*) **11**, 21, 60, **61**
Italy, invasion of 28, 54, 74–75

John (commander) 14, 32, 34, 36–37, 38, 40, 44, **45**, 46, 48–49, **50–51**, (52), 53, 71, 72
John the Armenian (commander) 32, 34, 38, 44, **45**, 48, 54
John the Cappadocian 6–7, 31, 42
John, brother of Pappus 60, **61**, **66–67**, (68), 69
Justin I (emperor) 54, 55
Justinian I (emperor) 4, 5, 5, 6–7, 8, 10, 11, **11**, 21–22, **21**, 26, 29, 30, 31, 37, 42, 54, 55, 57–58, 59, 65, 70, 73, 74, **74**, 75, 75, 76

Marcellus (commander) 14, 32, 44, **45**, 48, 65
Martinus (commander) 14, 29, 32, 38, 44, **45**, 48, 59, 62

Ortaïas (Berber leader) 60, **61**, 69
Ostrogoth forces 4, 5, 6, 55, 74

Pappas (commander) 14, 44, 45, 48, 60
Pharas (Heruli leader) 14, 53, 54, 55, 72

Sarapis (commander) 14, 65
Sardinia, fighting/forces in 6, 8, **9**, 14, 15, 22, 23, 38, 42, 43, 44, **45**, 47, **50–51**, (52), 54, 55, 73
Scalae Veteres, battle at 8, **9**, 26, 58, 60, 65, **66–67**, (68), 69, 74
  forces' strengths/dispositions 14, 27, 60, 61, **61**, **66–67**, (68), 69, 73
  tactics 28, 72
Sicily, forces/fighting on 8, **9**, 38, 54, 55, 59, 63, 64–65, 74
Sinnion (Hunnic commander) 14, 44, **45**
Solomon (commander) 14, 21, 22, 32, 38, 42, 57, 58–59, 59, 62, 63, 71
spearmen (*upaspistai*) 14–15, 48, 49, **64**
Stotzas (mutineers' leader) 8, 2, 58, 62, 65, 73, 75
  at Bagradas River 60, **61**, 63–64
  at Scalae Veteres 60, **61**, **66–67**, (68), 69

Tarasmundus (Gelimer's brother) 4, 5, 6, 55
Terentius (commander) 14, 65
Theodorus Cteanus (commander) 14, 21
Theodorus the Cappadocian (commander) 58, 59, 60, **61**, 62, 65, 69
Theudis (Visigoth ruler) 42, 54
Thracian forces 14, 15
Tricamarum, battle at 6, 8, **9**, 15, 41–44, **45**, 46–49, **50–51**, (52), 52–56, 70, 72, 73, 75
  forces' strengths/dispositions 14, 26, 27, 44, **45**, 47, 48–49, **50–51**, (52), 69
  tactics 26, 27, 48–49, (52), 72
Tzazon (Gelimer's brother) 8, 14, 15, 16, 23, 27, 42, 43, 44, **45**, 47, 48–49, 54, 72, 73

Uliaris (Belisarius' guard) 32, **33**, 39, 53

Valerian (commander) 14, 29, 32, 38, 44, **45**, 48
Vandal armies (cavalry) 4–6, 13, 14, 16, 17, 32, **33**, 48, 58, 60, **61**, 64, **66–67**, (68), 69
  armour/clothing 17, **18**, **19**, **23**, **26**, **27**, 28, **64**
  battle formations/tactics 27–28
  command of 15–16, 23, 24
  composition/strength 6, 15–17, 20, 23–24, 72
  helmets **18**, **19**, 28, 48, 49, **64**
  in Roman service 20, 22, 59, 73
  limitations of 16–17, 72, 73
  weapons/equipment 6, 16, 17, **18**, **19**, 23, **23**, 27, 28, 44, 48, **64**, **66–67**, (68), 72
Vandal Empire/Vandals (the)
  and Arian/Nicene Christianity 5, 6, 46, 54, 55, 57, 58, 59, 76, 77
  extent of 4, 5
  fall of 75, 76
  kingship/lineage 4–6
  reputation of 5, 31, 43, 76
  tribal affiliations/system 16, 24
Vandal navies 5, 72
Visigoths (the) 6, 42, 54

Witigis (Ostrogoth king) 54, 74

Zaidus (commander) 14
Zeno I, (emperor) 5, 22